Kaleidoscope of
Play Therapy Stories

Kaleidoscope of Play Therapy Stories

Edited by
Emily Oe and Sherrie Mullen

JASON ARONSON INC.
Northvale, New Jersey
London

This book was printed and bound by Book-mart of North Bergen, New Jersey.

The authors gratefully acknowledge permission to reprint the following: "The Little One," by Sherri Marshall Briggs, originally published in the *APT Newsletter* ©1991, 10(3); and "There Was a Tear," by Mike Mitchell, originally published in the *International Journal of Play Therapy*, ©1993, 2(1). Reprinted by permission of the Association for Play Therapy and the authors.

10 9 8 7 6 5 4 3 2 1

Library of Congress Cataloging-in-Publication Data.

Kaleidoscope of play therapy stories / edited by Emily Oe & Sherrie Mullen.
    p. cm.
    Includes bibliographical references and index.
    ISBN 1-56821-786-2
    1. Play therapy—Anecdotes. I. Oe, Emily. II. Mullen, Sherrie.
RJ505.P6K27   1996
616.89'1653—dc20   95-50408

Manufactured in the United States of America. Jason Aronson Inc. offers books and cassettes. For information and catalog write to Jason Aronson Inc., 230 Livingston Street, Northvale, New Jersey 07647.

INTRODUCTION

This kaleidoscopic collection of play therapy stories symbolizes the importance of the play therapy relationship in facilitating the client's free expression of feelings, thoughts, and actions with the consequent empowerment toward a more balanced integration of self. Furthermore, the power of shared experiences is valued in facilitating each person's unique impact on vivid individual and collective kaleidoscopic expression in the playroom and in the profession.

Until now, the stories were shared with only a few close friends and associates. Not all of the therapists, clients, and child artists are known; however, whoever they may be, they are acknowledged.

JUST A CHILD

I'm just a child—
Not very big,
Not very smart;
You look tremendous
   to me!
Like a tree in a forest,
Like a skyscraper
   in town, towering—
But . . . I'm just a child.

Because I'm a child
I make mistakes;
Plenty of them.
You look perfect to me,
Like a god in heaven,
Like a judge in court,
   condemning—
But me . . . I'm just
   a child.

And since I'm a child,
I am trusting.
I accept you totally.
You tell me what to do,
How to act, what
   to think.
Like I'm taught to do
I acquiesce, for I'm
   a good child.
Now I'm accepted
As the child I'm not.

Being just a child
Can be lonely,
Can be frightening.
I don't always know
   what to expect
From you.
Like a thunderous cloud,
Like a bolt of lightning
You strike . . . I'm
   scared, for I am
Only a child.

This little child
Needs assurance,
Needs acceptance.
I look at you and
   you're not there.

1

Your body is there,
Your never–ending
   work is there;

But your feelings stay
   somewhere
I know not,
Being the child I am.

Staying a child
Is painful,
Is frustrating.
Like you I want to be
   in control
Of the child that I am,
For in control I am not.

Can you see this child
Reaching out to touch,
Reaching out to share?
Not now, you say, this
   is important.
Not now, you say, don't
   be rude and interrupt.
Adults are fortunate
To be in such a
   good place
Unlike me, just a child.

As a child
I feel unimportant,
Just an extension of you;
But I fit in with everyone
   else

Following the same
   rules,
In the same way,
Wondering if I'll
   ever know
The child that is lost.

Can you hear me cry?
Do you know that
   I'm here?
Or do you accept that
This is how it is,
For it also happened
   to you?
And I fear I'll never grow
Like you, never knowing
   who I am,
Just a child. .   .   .

—*Cindy L. Wall*

BARBARA, 4

As Barbara was riding the car and visually exploring the room, she commented, "I wish this could be my room at home. I'd like to have all of these things but I can't have them." Head down, Barbara came toward me on the car. Then, lifting her head and looking *straight* at me, she said, "because of"—pointing her finger at me! The loving look in her eyes indicated how important this play therapy relationship was to her!!

—*Marcella McClain*

MRS. HORTON, 85

In explaining to another retirement home resident about play therapy, Mrs. Horton said, "I have to take something out of all this [play materials] and tell her [therapist] something about it. I haven't had too much trouble today. These little toys make me remember things. That's what play therapy is for!"

—*Debbie McDowell*

KATELYN, 7

On the way to session six, Katelyn let me know that Mom was going to bring her only every other week because it was so far to drive. During the session, her play was very different from previous sessions. Facing the puppet theater toward me, she wrote "THE LOST CHILD" on the board below and acted out a play where one puppet was *searching* for her daughter. After quite some time, the "parent" puppet finally found her daughter.

I clarified the schedule change with Katelyn's parents, and asked Katelyn how she felt about the change. She said she wanted to come every time, and her parents agreed because the school term was almost over. During the next session, Katelyn was back to her usual playroom activities.

—*Marianne Hampton*

NITA, 9

While we were waiting for Nita's mother, the following conversation occurred. "Nita, what are you going to do this afternoon?" *"I don't know."* "What are you going to do this weekend?" *"I don't know."* "What are you going to do 10 minutes from now?" *"I don't know."* "You're just not sure what you're going to do next." Eyes wide with sudden insight, Nita amazedly responded, "Yeah, *lots* of surprises!"

—*Tom Stevens*

TERESA, 7

I had four sessions with Teresa, a second grader. Due to scheduling difficulties and the referral concerns, I asked Teresa's permission to have her younger sister in grade one join us. Teresa agreed to share her playtime appointment with her sister. The next week, Teresa walked with me to Kerry's classroom, and the three of us went to my office. First to enter the room, Teresa went right to my chair and announced, "This is really my playroom, but I'll share it with you. In here, you can play and play, but sometimes Mrs. Lilley will say, 'Teresa, I know you are having fun with that,' and she'll tell you what you are doing but in an okay way. Then, she always says, 'Teresa, you may choose to do this or that.' Anyway, I think you'll like it in here with us."

—*Sheila Lilley*

TONY, 10

The setting was a residential treatment center. Tony was playing in the sandbox.

Tony: "Why do you always talk like that?"
Therapist: "You're curious about the way I talk."
Tony: "Really. Why *do* you talk like that?"
Therapist: "It seems to make you uncomfortable when I talk this way."
Tony: "No—it makes me feel important."

—*Judi Gilbert*

JERRY, 4

Jerry has been digging in the sandbox and has gotten sand in his sandals. He takes them off and brushes them clean "so Mom won't be angry." Then he brushes off his feet and begins scooting across the floor on his bare feet, finally deciding to put the shoes back on, but thinking he cannot do it by himself. He tries. He just can't get it. Help! I tell him to show me what he wants. He does, and we get the shoes back on THE WRONG FEET!! He doesn't care and neither do I.

—*Sherry Schultz*

AMANDA, 9

Amanda was the "secretary" of the school. After she had very knowledgeably relayed an intercom message to a teacher, the play therapist noted, "You really seem to know how to do that." Amanda offhandedly replied, "I should; I'm in the office enough."

—*Anonymous*

SHERRIE

One morning when I woke up, my husband asked, "Sherrie, did you know you talked in your sleep last night?" I was surprised and asked him what I said. He replied (in my sleeptalking words): "You're just lookin' around!"

—*Sherrie Mullen*

CASEY, 5

Casey was really testing the limits. He wanted to use the rubber mallet on something he could break, swinging it around different ways and watching himself in the one-way mirror. Casey got to the point where I felt that he was going to throw it at the mirror, so I set a limit. It was really hard for me to trust Casey when he said he wasn't going to throw the mallet, but I took him at his word and he didn't throw it!

—*Marianne Hampton*

CLINT, 7

The story was not new: divorce, father not turning up for visits. Clint engaged in stereotypical "boy" activities for several sessions. Then, one session, he lovingly and carefully wrapped a baby doll in a blanket, put it in his arm, and made several circles of the playroom as he "fed" the baby. Finally, Clint faced the therapist, and woefully asked, "Will I be a good daddy?"

—*Anonymous*

SHELLEY

Until I began to videotape my sessions, I never realized how quiet I was in the playroom. I have learned to be more verbal and to project my voice more. My tracking has a more consistent flow now without such long periods of silence.

—*Shelley Schenk*

DAVID, 7

As a home-based play therapist, I read David a story after play therapy. Being very tired this night, David climbed into his bed and said, "*You* tuck me in."

Me: "Oh, you want me to tuck you in tonight."
David: "Yep!"
Me: "Show me how."
David: "You know! Do it the way a mother does it."

—*Susan Corley*

MARCUS, 6

(This limit setting isn't so hard.) "Marcus, I know you want to do that, but the mirror is not for shooting." (Sounds all right so far!) "Okay?" (Did I *really* ask him if it's not okay to shoot at the mirror? Well, maybe I do need a bit more practice.)

—*Cindy Brownlow*

WESLEY, 6

As I met with my elementary students at the beginning of the school year, first-grader Wesley ran up to me, ready for a counseling session in the playroom. I explained to him that I would come and get him after lunch. This formerly very quiet child looked rather crestfallen that I could not see him immediately. Wesley finally looked up at me and very softly said, "Okay, but will you miss me?"

—*Kay Collier*

MARY

What a thrill I have when the child client expresses the meaning of the playroom by asking the questions "Do other children come here?", "Who all comes here to play?", or "Do you play with lots of kids?" One of the most touching moments is when the child turns back to the room at the end of the the session and says, "Goodbye, room" with a wistfulness as if the longing is there to stay in that safety longer.

—*Mary Ring*

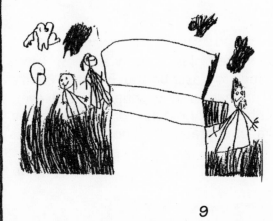

BENJAMIN, 7

During sandplay, Benjamin placed different animal figures in strategic places. Putting two identical figures face to face, he looked up at me and whispered, "They're doing the 'F' word." Though I was shocked that he knew about the "F" word, I calmly responded, "Oh, they're doing the 'F' word." Benjamin continued in his play, unaware of what was going on in *my* mind! However, I really was surprised about three minutes later when again he turned to me and whispered, "They're Fighting!" I learned that day not to assume to know what a child is thinking!

—*Sally Creed*

MARGE

During my first supervised play therapy session, I frequently used "working" to describe much of the child's activity—most often an inaccurate description. However, I can certainly describe what *I* did as *work*. Play therapy is an art, and takes a lot of practice. I'll be "working" at it for a long time!

—*Marge Heath*

ANNA, 3

Anna was referred for suspected sexual abuse. Session after session, she threw toys over her shoulder, emptied the shelves and containers, and several times tested and ignored the limits to the point of choosing to leave the playroom. Her language was sexual and profane. I began to dread the sessions, knowing I would be there for at least 30 minutes cleaning up, but I also knew something important was going on within Anna. After a while, her play was more calm, and she began to engage me in more activities, often moving my chair and instructing me in how to play with her. Then, one day while we were making butterflies with  playdough, Anna leaned over to me and said, "My daddy is a scuzbum." I cried that day at realizing how I had been entrusted with a child's confidence.

—Judy Owens

MRS. GRAVES, 83

Leaving her room for our session, Mrs. Graves said to her roommate, "Well, I'll be back. We're going to play for a while!"

—Debbie McDowell

CHRIS, 7

When I think of the play therapy I have had the privilege to do with children, what I remember most are the wonderful transitions where I see that maybe miracles do happen! Of course, these "miracles" are wrought by the complete acceptance of the child by the play therapist.

One such "miracle" occurred with Chris, who was referred to therapy due to aggressive behavior and stealing. He began play therapy by hoarding all the blocks to make his fort, leaving me with only a few men and a few blocks with which to "battle" (at his direction) his entire army. Across sessions, these battles decreased and I was given a more equal number of men and blocks. Our "sides" began a peaceful coexistence. Later, the army men were no longer brought out for play (Chris told me they were now farmers). The separate forts became one huge "castle" that we built together, where Chris had a prince and princess live. And—would you believe it?— these themes in his play mirrored his behaviors outside the playroom, where his aggressive behavior had declined to where he was now described as "cooperative and happy."

So, yes, Virginia, miracles really can happen in play therapy! And when they do, *hold onto them and cherish them!*
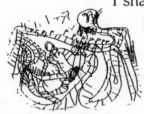
I share this story with other play therapists often, and it rekindles my hope and passion for the job that I do. After all, how many jobs are there where someone can say: "You know, I was part of a miracle!"

—*Jamie Langley*

THERE WAS A TEAR

There was a tear.
It was wet.
It was salty.
It had a home, in a body, in an eye.
It had a beginning, in a heart,
    in a feeling, in a soul.
The tear had a job, a messenger
    in a sob.
The messages were meant to
    speak to many, inside and out.
Some heard, inside and out,
    and the tear would disappear,
    approved of by those
    who accepted its message.
Others ignored its message,
    dooming the tear to repeat its slide,
    hugging the cheek and falling
    to make silent pools of sad/happy messages
    crying to be heard.
There was a tear, which lived with a fear
    that no one was near,
    and in the soul, would grow old.
A pearl in a shell.
A bottomless well.

—*Mike Mitchell*

From: *International Journal of Play Therapy*, 2(1), 1993.

ALLAN, 4

In our play therapy course practice sessions, Allan (non-client) was in the playroom for his third time, each time with a different student therapist. He asked, "What do you want me to paint?" The therapist replied, "In here, you can decide." That freedom and personal responsibility seemed to be just too much for Allan. He stepped aside from the easel, hands to forehead and then into wide gestures as he adamantly said, "You all say I can color what I want . . . I can say what I want . . . I can do what I want. Oh–h–h–h, I'm *dizzy* of all that!!"

—*Emily Oe*

BOBBY, 5

At the end of a particularly active play therapy session, Bobby threw his arms around this therapist and said, "I love you!"

—*Sidney Pozmantier*

TIM, 6

Tim brought me cookies and said, "You know why I brought you these cookies that I made for you? Because you help me with my feelings. I can be mad, sad, or glad, and it sure is a lot better to be glad. So, I brought you these cookies, and (putting his hand over his heart) these are from my good heart to yours!"

—*Jeanette Mallory*

SHERRI

The experience of a relationship developed through play therapy has been life-changing for me. Watching this relationship grow, change, and become something real was a mysterious revelation. I was not equipped for such an experience. After 10 sessions with one child, I realized that a bond had formed without any manipulation, planning, or control on my part. The freeing up of all the tendencies to flatter, compliment, bribe, or other ways of getting a child to cooperate was wonderful. My small client was bonding with me because I had accepted him and had given him permission to be himself. I felt that a miracle had occurred not unlike the birth of a new baby. He was a different person than when the relationship had started. I was different, also. Nondirective play therapy allows the client much freedom to attempt self-actualization. I have seen it happen, and I want to be a part.

—*Sherri Marshall Briggs*

PETER, 6

After each session, Peter would ask for a Coke as we passed the kitchen area. I would respond, "You really know what you would like, but all I have is water. You can choose that if you wish." Each week, he would get a cup and fill it with water. Finally, on one occasion, he said, "Now, while I drink this, I want you to watch and say what you see me doing." I did, and I also taught his mother how to track behavior! He was a kiddo who knew what he liked!

—*Karen Hudson*

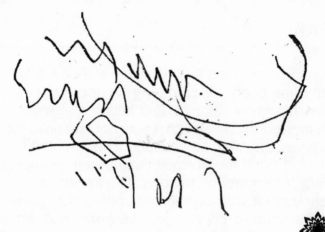

NEDA, 4

Neda spilled the sand on the floor.
Therapist: "We will clean it later."
Neda: "My parents always spill their feelings."

—*Doris Omdahl*

16

IAN, 5

My time came to find out how I would react when a child aimed a dart gun at me. Ian shot the dart gun at *many* things in the playroom, including *me*. When he shot it over my head, I thought that wasn't so bad. With his hands *and* feet handcuffed to the leg of the easel, he skillfully lifted the gun and started shooting darts around my legs. All of a sudden, Ian released one dart that struck my chest. I remarked, "Oh, that surprised you! It hit me right here." He said, "Right in the heart!" and I realized that perhaps I should have set a limit on his aiming the gun. However, somehow I felt that Ian need-ed to release that dart at someone and since he was not really trying to hurt me, I would let it pass. Ian went on to something else and gave me the courage to let a child feel free and the strength to let him take responsibility for his actions.

—Pat Ledyard

MICKY, 3

Micky was such a tiny boy. He tried so desperately to get a toy from an upper shelf. I could see he was getting frustrated, choosing other toys but continually staring at the one on the upper shelf. I wanted so terribly to get that toy for Micky, but managed with the greatest exer-tion of willpower to refrain from getting it for him. Toward the end of the session, he finally managed to get the toy. Never was I more relieved *or* proud! Through this experience, I learned more to respect and to allow even the smallest children to struggle. The smile of success on Micky's face was worth my self-restraint.

—Tina Nunnellee

MARY JOY, 8

Four months after termination, Mary Joy wanted to come back to play therapy. She explained her painting to the therapist: "This is the sun saying 'HI' to the shark. You're the sun, and I'm the shark." Even though she and the therapist had parted amiably, Mary Joy still seemed unsure that things would be the same. However, in the next session, she described another painting: "This is a heart-person saying 'HI' to you; I'm the heart-person."

—*Anonymous*

BARRY, 4

Barry had painted a picture in his previous session, leaving it in the playroom. In this session, he was very upset upon not finding it where he had left it. Instead of getting his picture for him, I just tracked his feelings and thoughts during his struggle to find his picture. Finally, Barry decided to paint a replacement picture. This experience reaffirmed my belief in children solving their own problems. I am very glad that I had the self-control and facilitative responses that Barry needed to solve his "missing picture dilemma."

—Jennifer Rodes

MISSY, 6

Missy was referred due to aggressive behavior toward her parents and a friend. It became evident that she manipulated her mother to get her own way. During one session, Missy spilled some sand that she was "cooking for dinner." Later, she slipped on it and fell lightly on her hip. She looked at me, smiled, and then began to cry. I asked if she had hurt herself. She nodded, pointed to her hip, and said, "I want my Mommy." I replied, "At first, you smiled, and then you started to cry." Missy repeated her request, and I said, "That must have really scared you to fall in here." She immediately stopped crying, sat down, and appeared to be quietly thinking. After a moment, Missy returned to her play. I believe Missy was more embarrassed than scared. However, I realize that, through this experience, she was able to increase her self-confidence, self-control, and ability to work through challenges for herself.

—Donald (Mac) McGuire

SHERRY

One of my biggest problems in play therapy revolves around limit setting. Imagine that! Limit setting is my biggest *life problem*, and here it raises its ugly head in the playroom. Learning to set limits comfortably at the last possible moment and believing that I actually have a right to set limits is a big step for me—nay, dare I say, it is more like a pole vault for me. My discomfort with limit setting makes me nervous and fearful that I am doing the wrong thing—that I may get hurt or that I may inadvertently hurt others inside and outside the playroom.

—Sherry Jones

ZACHARY, 7

A father brought his son, Zachary, to play therapy and stayed for the entire session! This was a father who was adamantly against his child being in therapy, especially play therapy. He had told his wife he would divorce her if she took *his* son to play therapy. After a year with further problems, the mother brought Zachary without the father's knowledge. After three sessions, she told him. By then, he could see some positive changes in Zachary's behavior and agreed to bring him to a session.

When Dad got home after this session, Mom asked what he thought, and he replied, "Well, to tell the truth, I feel like I just spent an hour with Mrs. Rogers." I took that as a true compliment!

—Jeanette Mallory

JOEY, 7

After serving as a volunteer for the beginning play therapy class, my son Joey delightedly concluded (as he was leaving the clinic), "Mom, I really freaked out those teachers!" The next day (after saying nothing more about the play therapy experience), Joey approached his father to ask for an expensive toy. When his father explained that the family would not be able to purchase the toy, Joey thoughtfully responded, "Well, I guess the play therapist would say, 'You look really disappointed.'" Little did I realize that, in three 25-minute mini-practicum sessions, Joey would recognize and learn how to use an appropriate play therapy response!

—*Vicki LeMay*

NICK, 6

As I tracked Nick in my first play therapy session, he insisted, "I want to know what time it is, and I want to leave this room. It has baby toys." Nick continually asked what time it was. He did not want to move. He only talked about leaving and what time it was. This was difficult for me as Nick spoke negatively about the playroom, and I found tracking his comments a definite challenge. However, I followed him, and at the end of the session, Nick picked up the knife. He *did* find something in the playroom that interested him, so it seemed he did not find the room completely inappropriate after all.

—*Julie Stafford*

JUSTIN, 8

Justin expressed anxiety over the video camera soon after entering the playroom, and his concern grew as the session progressed. He repeatedly used a shark puppet to attack the small window behind which the camera was placed; he also shot at the camera and made stabbing gestures with the knife. Justin draped rubber snakes over the curtain rod above the window that housed the camera. He propped an impressive display of defenses on a table next to the window including the gun and knife both propped on blocks and traffic signs ("STOP" and "SPEED LIMIT"). *Finally*, Justin placed a square Lego platform on the windowjamb, obscuring the camera's view *completely*!

—*Sylvia Kidd*

JEANNE, 5

Jeanne was enjoying talking on the toy phone in the playroom when she turned toward me holding up one finger and nodding, as if to say, "I'll be right with you!" At that point, Jeanne turned away from me, lowered her voice and said, "I have to go now. I'm in therapy."

—*Ann Grassfield*

ALEJANDRO, 5

As expected when I arrived at the classroom door, the teacher remarked, "Oh, thank goodness you're here. You can have him." Alejandro looked at me and rolled his eyes. After we got outside the door, I commented, "Looks like you didn't like that very much." Very seriously, Alejandro responded, "Do you think when we come back you could take *her* to the playroom?"

—*James Flowers*

JAKE, 5

After his play therapy session, Jake told his mother, "I'm just so tired! I played just as hard as I could today." His mother replied, "Sounds like you were really busy today." Musingly, Jake declared, "Yes, this must be how Daddy feels after he works all day."

—*Sherree Murray*

REMINGTON, 15

In my work as an adaptive behavior teacher in a high school behaviorist program, one student stands out as a child most in need of play therapy. Remington suffered from fetal alcohol effect, *said* he had smoked cigarettes since conception, and if he was not active, fell asleep. One afternoon while the other students and I gathered around the table to compete in a board game, he laid his chair back-down on the floor and then put his legs over the chair seat with his head on the floor. Remington commenced to twitch, loll his head to one side, and make short barking sounds like a squirrel. I was not sure if he was pretending, having *petit mal* seizures, or . . . ? "Naw," said Remington. "I'm going into the dead parts of my brain."

I am fond of wearing Birkenstock shoes, and Remington found my brown clogs especially unattractive. He called them "shit-stomping shoes." One day, during his usual disruption on his way to the time-out room to nap, he must have felt more kindly toward me than usual. I had on my clogs, and Remington said with some glee, "Come on, Miss, let's go stomp in some dog shit." This time he included me in his play rather than setting me up as the target of his abuse. It seemed that we had made a connection through our play experiences together. Just imagine what actual play therapy would offer for Remington!

—*Sandy Carter*

MADDIE, 4

Maddie made her way around the playroom, softly speaking as she engaged briefly in a variety of activities. She did not seem to pay much attention to the therapist's tracking until the therapist said, "I'm not sure what you're saying, but I can hear you speaking." It was like magic. Maddie looked up from her painting and began telling her entire story loudly, a story laden with strong issues. There was such a difference in Maddie's behavior before and after the statement, as though she could not believe that this grown person would want to listen to her, although it was clear that she needed *so much* to be heard.

—*Stephanie Stevens*

LAUREN, 7

For several weeks, Lauren used the doctor's kit to repair the therapist's heart and to give her medicine to make her well. She also would pretend to cut open her own chest and take out her "bad" heart. Then, one day, Lauren "opened" her chest and announced: "See, it's getting better. It's not a bad heart, just a broken heart. You're going to make it better—*we're* going to make it better!"

—*Carolyn Adams*

JADE, 6; JASON, 3

Jade was having a difficult time adjusting to her new baby brother. It was difficult to change from being the only child to sharing her parents. By the time her brother Jason was 3 years old, the sibling rivalry was in full bloom. They had taken to sneaking up and attacking each other. This finally led the parents to bring them for play therapy. Conceptualizing children from an Adlerian perspective, I recommended sibling therapy. I sensed that Jade was experiencing being a dethroned first child. Jason was able to express this in his own special way through play. He put on the crown, placed a baby bottle in his mouth, and strutted around the playroom, saying, "I'm the Baby-King!"

—*Linda Homeyer*

KEVIN, 5

 First time in the playroom, Kevin touched everything. It was apparent how special he felt as he stated, "This is all just for me!!" After a few minutes of exploring, Kevin slipped into fantasy play. However, when the 5-minute time was given, Kevin again made sure he touched everything in the room before he left.

—Peggy Heath

JAYNE, 4

On the way to the playroom, Jayne seemed pretty scared, dodging tall adults and looking down the long hallway, thumb in mouth and eyes as round as saucers. I just wanted to pick her up and tell her that everything was going to be okay. When we got to the playroom, I could see a look of uncertainty and hope that something familiar would be on the other side of the door. At that point, I opened the door and said, "Jayne, this is our playroom and in here you can do many of the things you want." Her eyes lit up and she immediately began to explore the room. Just seeing the look on her face, I felt as though I actually did reach down and tell her that everything was going to be okay, but she didn't need me to do that. She was just fine now.

—Tommy Wilbeck

LITTLE BOY'S TAIL

Precious little boy
In your own little world
Where tigers jump
Their tails in a twirl.

Brave little one
Bearing all of your pain
Yet no tears come—
Crying's in vain.

Frightened little child
Brought to a healing place
Left in a playroom
With a friendly face.

Busy little boy
With a Slinky in tow
Lying in a sandbox
Striped puppets in a row.

Loved little soul
By that bright-eyed girl
Will you lock yourself out,
Or speak in *her world*?

Accepted little one
Your eyes meet hers
When she utters *your* word
Then you are sure.

Happy little boy
Humming a Pooh-song
Hopping on a Tigger-tail
Coming right along.

Little play therapy boy
With the help of the
play-girl,
Bring your beloved tail
As you step into *her* world.

—*Kimberly M. Dillon*

TONYA, 6

First grader Tonya repetitively enacted scenarios where the students were in trouble—seemingly without justification and resulting in names on the chalkboard and other consequences. In a despairing voice and with tilted head, she remarked one day, "I just don't know what's wrong with Johnny *this* year; he was such a *good* kid *last* year." After many sessions, she was addressing her confusion over her own school performance—a young girl with 2–3 petit mal seizures a minute—and finding first grade so much more difficult than kindergarten. However, with this admission, she seemed to feel more in control and announced, "You know, you can get your name on the board for doing something good, too!"

—*Anonymous*

BRANDON, 5

Brandon, who had been sexually abused for many years, repeatedly played out his need for protection using a small Fisher-Price dollhouse. In fantasy play, the little people set up wooden blocks around the exterior of their house and then set up traps to hinder or hurt the perpetrator on the outside. After a number of sessions, the people gained victory over the perpetrator, never again to be threatened by him. Then, in the next session, the child created a new structure out of the wooden blocks: a stun-

ning, perfectly symmetrical "castle" in place of the home that had to be protected previously. What a beautiful symbol of his new sense of security—which he had created *for himself* through his own fantasy play!

When this child arrived for his final session, he brought a camera so his mother could take a picture of him and me. Again, how symbolic of the importance of the therapeutic relationship that I was important enough to warrant a photograph when, during his first *two* sessions, he cried, screamed, called me names, hit and kicked me—not wanting to be there with me—and seldom interacting with me throughout our sessions!

—*Theresa Fusaro*

SAMUEL, 7

Samuel first came to the playroom as a noncommunicative, frightened second-grader. He had rages in the classroom and tried to run away from his teachers. When given an assignment, Samuel would cry with frustration and rock in his chair.

Gradually, Samuel relaxed in the playroom and acted out several traumatic events in his life. He loved to create music and to create dramas with the puppets and dolls. As his trust grew, Samuel began to participate in classroom activities and to take pride in his work.

By the end of the school year, Samuel said he wished that school was all year long. He played a "special tune" on the xylophone for his counselor so she "wouldn't forget him over the summer," hugged her, and rushed out the door.

—*Anonymous*

JEREMIAH, 7

Jeremiah had many therapists and many placements since age 2. He was an extremely bright child who had committed numerous violent acts against family members, home, and possessions. Also, he was noted to be suspicious of therapists and resistant to most treatment approaches.

In the first session, Jeremiah stood silently, arms folded, lower lip stuck out, glowering, with only more defiant looks in response to my reflections. I was thinking rapidly.

> What if he does this the whole session? His mother is paying for this. What if he tells her all we did was sit and do *nothing*? But if, by my actions, I push for some action, then I will have indicated that he really can't do "almost anything he wants." And, he's so mistrustful of therapists already— probably with good reason. He's certainly experienced more than his share of them. He's really kind of proud and vulnerable at the same time standing there like that. What do I do?

I sat there watching this wonderfully determined and very hurt little boy, and contemplated the possibilities of Jeremiah's mother "firing me" before I had a chance to see what Jeremiah was all about. However, I was committed to the child-centered concept of letting Jeremiah "do almost anything he wanted to do"—standing silently and glaring straight ahead of him for the entire 45 minutes. In fact, I rather admired him for the stance that he was taking! My verbal reflections to Jeremiah during that session included, "We've been in here together for 45 minutes and you have moved *only* twice. I'm not sure, but I think you may be the only person who has ever done that."

In successive sessions, Jeremiah continued to be guarded and seemingly cautious on matters pertaining to trust, but there was no repeat of the "silent session." Discussing his progress several months later, Jeremiah's mother related the following:

> That first time I brought Jeremiah, he was so angry at me. He didn't want to come to another therapist. He was mad because he wasn't seeing his former therapist, and he was mad because you're a "girl." In the car driving home, I finally asked him, "Well, how did it go?" He looked disdainfully at me and finally answered *with pride and triumph in his voice*, "Huh! I stood in one spot for 45 minutes, and I only moved my foot once and scratched my nose once—and I'm the only one who has ever done that!"

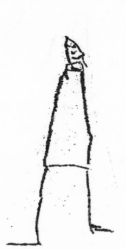

I believe that Jeremiah showed me in his own way what is so strongly purported as the "necessary and sufficient conditions" of the therapeutic relationship in child-centered play therapy. By attending to my discomfort as well as my growing respect for this proud and angry little boy, I was able to convey to Jeremiah, in a way that he could perceive, what I was experiencing with him, and he was able to more fully *experience* the therapeutic process.

—*Sandra Frick-Helms*

RUSSELL, 4

Blond, blue–eyed, cherub–faced,
  entered my classroom and
  my heart.

Angry, sad, frustrated,
  Violent!

Time, patience, space,
  Pressure lifted.
  Love entered.
  Eyes twinkle.
  Hugs given,
  on his terms.

A new home assigned,
  tears,
  good–byes said.
  Will love last?

—*Lois Stark*

CONNIE, 5

Connie was struggling to make sense of the custody battle that stormed all around her. Currently, her parents had joint custody, and she rotated weekly living with Mom or Dad. So as Connie tried to figure this all out, her play reflected the struggle. Connie repeatedly directed me to participate in joint family play. Her puppet family had a dad, a mom, and a baby. My family, selected by Connie, had a dad, a mom, and a baby who was a dog puppet. Play always turned to her having something terrible happen to my family. In one session, my family became vampires. I had to work hard, as directed by Connie, to try to save my family. However, every time I followed directions, Connie would either change the rules or steal away the magical healing objects.

This play continued until Mom prematurely terminated Connie's play therapy. Connie had stopped her suicidal ideation that brought her into therapy, so Mom thought she was "cured."

It was hard not having Connie return. She had been doing such hard, productive work. From my perspective, her safe place was no longer available to her to try to figure out how her family, which had been a good place to live, had now somehow changed into good and bad places.

Not all our cases have happy endings. However, most are memorable because of the persevering spirit in children.

—*Linda Homeyer*

PATRICK, 8

Play therapy often maintains a mystical quality that defies explanation. Exactly how change occurs often seems to fall into the realm of speculation. Over the years, Patrick has been an inspiration to my students and me about not giving up on a child, whether the therapist understands what changes are taking place or not.

Patrick was described by his teacher as an "occasional student," who attended class about two to three times per week. When the school social worker had tried to make contact with the family, no one was home. I agreed to see Patrick "the next time he comes to school." I was called away from another school early one morning because Patrick had dropped into school for at least half of the day. I found a bedraggled, ragamuffin child with dirty blond hair and rumpled clothes. His face and hands were clean. We went to the playroom immediately with me explaining that the playroom was a place Patrick could do many of the things he wanted to do. I opened the door and took my position in the adult chair.

Patrick immediately pulled a child's chair into the middle of the floor and wrapped his legs around the chair legs. There he sat, looking down at the floor and saying nothing. I continued to reflect what I thought were his feelings of loneliness, fear, and uneasiness. Patrick remained unresponsive and unmoved. He missed the rest of the week of school.

Promptly on the play therapy day, Patrick was in school. I went to his room and escorted him to the playroom. He talked to me about the games he liked, his friends, and the important things in his life. At the playroom door, he grew silent. Remaining silent, Patrick again took his position in the chair in the middle of the room. Thus, the theme was set for eight weeks of Patrick's silence and my agony over what I was doing wrong. I gave up and reported to the teacher that this was one child I could not get through to in order to help him.

The teacher looked at me and said, "You can't stop seeing Patrick. He is up to grade level. He never misses school anymore, and he has so many friends in our class. It's a miracle what you have done with him."

I returned with Patrick to the playroom—and he sat. I did other work, giving him the occasional reflection. I tried to take him outside and get him to talk. Nothing worked. Thirty-two sessions later, Patrick was still silent in the playroom.

The next year Patrick was in another school in the district. He rarely missed school. Nine years later, Patrick graduated from high school. I do not know what changed him, but I do know that it was some magic that took place in the playroom. I know that we shared it, but I do not know what it was. Patrick's message across these years has been that understanding by the therapist is not necessary for therapy to take place.

—*Karla Carmichael*

STEPHANIE, 8

As a beginning play therapist, I had a preconceived idea about how children would act in the playroom. I thought we would go in, play, and see overt evidence of some significance in the child's play, but Stephanie was different. For 12 weeks, she came in and played with the sandbox, sifting the sand and putting it into different containers. Sometimes, she would use this sand in the kitchen to cook something, and while it was cooking, she would go to the easel and paint. Stephanie seemed to do this week after week. I would just sit in my chair and track what she did and reflect the few feelings that she would show because she hardly ever said a word.

The next to the last session, Stephanie got angry while painting at the easel. Then, when we were walking back to the waiting room, I reminded her that next week would be our last session and she slumped her shoulders, hung her head, and had tears in her eyes. I had not known that our relationship had such an impact on her. I actually thought Stephanie was indifferent about the whole thing even though her mother told me that she just loved coming. I thought that she might have just said that because she got out of school early on Wednesdays. I was so surprised by the effect I had on this little 8-year-old girl by just being present in the room with her and totally accepting her for who she was.

—*Malorie Hanks*

BEVERLY

I have learned that the hardest tracking is the child coming into the playroom and doing nothing—overtly. I have to sit there and repeatedly track the eye movement, finger/hand movement, and just basically anything I can find. However, I have learned that just keeping verbally with the child and accepting the child as he/she is in the moment may be the most important interaction.

—Beverly Lilie

LYDELL, 6

Lydell questioned me about when he could begin his play sessions at home (filial therapy).

Me: "That is something your parents will have to decide."
Lydell: "Just like I get to decide in here."

—Judi Gilbert

GARY, 3

Gary's favorite playroom activity was being "G. I. Joe" or "Rambo." Then, after an unexplained four-week absence, he entered the playroom and threw the guns on the floor, stating, "I don't like guns!" He swept many items off the shelves and exhaustedly collapsed on the floor.

Finally, Gary got up (as in a daze) and climbed into the clothes trunk with a knife and a gun. After several stealthy attempts to raise the closed lid with the rubber knife blade, he threw the lid up with both the knife and the gun, and exclaimed, "There, I got out!!" Later, Gary's mother shared information that fit the picture. Gary had just experienced the third family death in a year: a 21-year-old cousin with cancer the previous December, Grandfather with a stroke in October, and an uncle who shot himself this December. No wonder the child was confused! It took many sessions of "death" scenarios before Gary seemed to feel in control of his life again.

—*Anonymous*

40

THE KEY

Take the key
Open the way
Unlock my mind
Free my misconceptions
Remove the pain
Show me worth.

Take the key
Open the way
Release my heart
Break through the walls of protection
Liberate my emotions
Empower me.

Give me the key to open the way.
Reveal its shape and appearance
Allow me to open my way,
Gain worth
Empower
Experiment with choice.

The key's appearance is vague,
The shape is formless,
Yet, in grasping, the way is revealed.
The pain is lessened
Walls erode
Power comes
Worth recognized.

—Sherri Marshall Briggs

STEVEN, 3

Steven's mother struggled with explaining the merits of play therapy to the child's skeptical granddad. As time passed, Granddad saw improvements in Steven's behavior and was excited. Mom decided to caution Granddad that at times, Steven's behavior may improve and at other times, it may regress. Granddad said, "Oh, don't worry about that! It's kinda like being on a diet—you lose a little, you gain a little—but it all works out."

—*Sherrie Mullen*

ADAM, 4

Adam shot the dart above the shelves and cabinet. He had this surprised look like "Uh–oh!" He stood there and then said, "I guess I'm going to have to go up there and get it" but the expression on his face said, "I'm really not going to be able to get this down. What am I going to do?" When I acceptingly acknowledged his concern without any pressure to retrieve the dart, he seemed to relax and just said, "Oh, well" before moving on to another activity.

—*Beverly Lilie*

KAYLEEN, 8; MEENA, 7

In sibling group play therapy, Meena and Kayleen really exemplified the uniqueness of sibling relationships.

M: "Kayleen, are we gonna tell Mom what we did today?"

K: "No!"

Th: "So, you're planning together what you're going to tell Mom."

M: "Because we're sisters."

Th: "Sounds like you think sisters should work together."

M: "We always work together at home. Whatever my sister does, I do, and whatever I do, my sister does."

K: "Liar—sometimes we fight!"

—*Stephanie Stevens*

PAUL, 6

Paul was busy in the sandbox, moving the sand around, building and destroying, scooping and dumping. He had been busy at work for some time without any verbal interaction with the play therapist. After a while, Paul looked over to the play therapist and said, "You know, coming here is more fun than watching Bart Simpson!"

—*Linda Homeyer*

CRAIG, 5

The 2½–foot punching bag seemed just the right size for Craig session after session. Having witnessed his grandfather and father beating his grandmother three years previously, it appeared that Craig was now releasing his anger and confusion.

One day, Craig discovered a pair of adult scissors accidentally left in the playroom. Immediately, he attacked the punching bag, repeatedly stabbing it and saying "I'm gonna get you!" Finally, the bag was deflated, and I said, "You really got that. You seem really angry." Craig's eyes got BIG, as if saying, "Someone finally heard me!" He then proceeded to cut up the deflated bag, putting the pieces in a paper bag and stating victoriously, "I'm taking this home with me!!"

With Craig, in that time of our relationship, there was never a question of limiting the destruction of the punching bag. I knew that Craig's safety and freedom to express himself in that way was more important than the cost of the bag for me.

—*Carolyn Adams*

KIM, 5

Love is not enough. Of course, we bring our love to our work but also all of our training, skills, and experience. Recently, I had a particularly chaotic session with Kim. Paints were thrown all around the room, a tub of water was overturned, the shelves were cleared in one wild swing of her arms. (The carpet will never be the same!) She repeatedly tried to destroy other toys, even her favorite bunny. She told me how much she hated me and did not like the way I talked or the way I wore my hair. However, Kim did not want to leave the playroom when the session was over!

I questioned myself about what I did or did not do and wondered about what would have been a more appropriate way to help this child who has no tolerance for frustration. The next day I called Mom, who reported that Kim had a wonderful evening at home and slept well. Before going to sleep, Mom read her a story and they talked about the session. Kim again said she did not like me, or my hair, or the way I talk. Then, she related the paint incident. Mom suggested she might want to apologize to me next week. Kim replied, "Oh, I don't have to do that! She loves me."

Sometimes, maybe love is enough!

—*Jeanette Mallory*

CARLA, 10

After Carla's sexual molestation, her mother brought her to our state and abandoned her. In our group of children who had been sexually abused, Carla was quite evasive about the abuse, seemingly hanging on with pride and denial but no disclosure. In my directive group play therapy session one night, I decided to play the "Snow Picture Game." When it was Carla's turn, as if a switch was flipped OPEN, she pointed nonchalantly to different pieces of colorful packing foam and described the scene in the attic where she was molested. She described the cot where she was placed, the cigarette she was offered, the open window where she threw away the cigarette, the single light bulb, the storage boxes and car parts that were also in the attic. As Carla permitted herself to talk about those things more, she began to swallow hard, tears welled up in her eyes, and her voice broke. At the end of her disclosure, an exhausted Carla just put her head on the crook of her elbow and cried uncontrollably. Gaining a genuine feeling of safety, Carla started her healing process that day—all because of a handful of simple packing foam.

—*Norma Leben*

AMBER, 4

In the second session, Amber used the play telephone to enact an intensely emotional conversation with someone she referred to as "boss." Scolding the "boss" for not listening to her, she threatened to wash the boss's *ears* out with soap and said, "You never listen to me, Mom!" Realizing her slip of the tongue, she stopped and whispered aside to me, "The boss is my mom." There was a pause in her phone conversation as though she were listening. Then, she responded in a serious tone, "I'm at the doctor's—*playing*, of course!"

Over the course of the first four sessions, Amber further expressed her dawning view of the therapeutic relationship. In the initial session, she said, "I want you to get used to me." During the third session, she spontaneously turned away from her play and remarked, "You're such a silly little doctor!" In the fourth session, she stated, "You're a nice doctor. I like you," adding very thoughtfully, "You're a doctor to play with, not a doctor to talk to."

—*Christina Palmer*

Child Protective Services had determined that Chelsy and her 5-year-old brother could return to live with their mother after a temporary placement with an aunt. Chelsy was ready, but her brother did not want to go. Chelsy wrote this note to her brother at home and brought it to her play therapy session to share with me. (Chelsy did stay with her aunt for two more weeks before she went back with her mother; her brother went back two more weeks after that.)

—*Judi Gilbert*

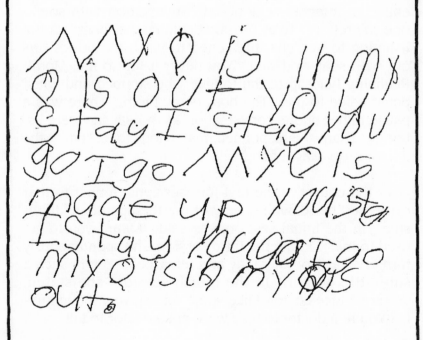

LEANNA, 10

•••

During my basic play therapy course, I was ever so eager to apply what I had been learning to my everyday life—translated: I used my daughter as my guinea pig. As the semester progressed, my Leanna learned that she could choose and make her own decisions; she learned that Mom could set limits; she even learned that I was not going to do things for her that she was capable of doing herself. *What I was unaware of was that I was the one fixing to learn a valuable lesson!*

One day as we were baking cupcakes, Leanna decided that she would fill the large cupcake tins and I would do the small ones. Having completed her part, Leanna motioned for me to do my part. I eagerly took over; holding the large metal bowl with both hands, I began pouring batter into the tins. Immediately, too much batter came pouring out causing the pan to tip over and the batter to flow all over the pan, all creating a nice little mess. Immediately, I called out for Leanna to help me. I had intended for her to put her arms around me and put the pan back upright. Instead, she just stood there. I looked over at her only to catch her grinning. Before I could say anything, Leanna simply said, "Don't do for the adult what the adult can do for herself!"

LESSON LEARNED!

—Jaye Kelly

49

PENNY, 4

Penny struggled with the marital problems of her mother and stepfather for 11 sessions, including ending several sessions by "drawing" a forest with a bad wolf chasing a mother and her little girl. In the 12th session, Penny started by drawing the forest with the wolf, mother, and little girl all walking happily together. She then played brief bits of her play themes in the previous 11 sessions and concluded by lying in the bean bag and pretending to be a baby peacefully cuddled in a blanket with bottle in mouth.

—*Anonymous*

ROBIN, 6

As a novice play therapist, I always wonder if what I say in the playroom is correct and if the child really hears me. I was tracking Robin on every move she made to make sure I was getting her feelings and thoughts. When Robin put a lobster in front of my face, I astutely observed, "You really want me to see that." "Yeah," she said. She came closer and closer, and finally put the claw up my nose, seemingly right up to my sinus cavity! I set a limit! Robin laughed, looked right at me, and said, "Seems like you don't like that." I guess she hears *everything*!

—*James Flowers*

RANDY, 6

During an in-home play therapy session with Randy, who was ill, the phone rang. Typical of a child his age, Randy jumped up to answer the phone. From his responses, it was obvious that the adult on the other end was trying to engage him in conversation. Randy gave the caller several one-word responses and then said, "You'll have to talk to my mom; I've got playing to do here!" He knew the value of time!

—*Judy Webb*

DUSTIN, 4

Dustin asked me for a glass of water. After I responded, "In here, you can help yourself," Dustin said, "When *you* come to *my* house, I'm not getting you nothin'!"

—*Robin Lee*

CARL, 12

After my play therapy training, I realized that I could change my verbal approach in all of my counseling. Carl, who had been coming regularly, noticed the change immediately: "Oh, I get it. Now, you're doing that counseling thing." I wonder what he thought we were doing in our previous sessions!

—*Terri Evensvold*

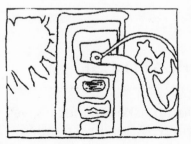

BRETT, 9

In the second session, Brett was still establishing the relationship with the therapist. Brett painted a picture of the office building in which the counseling center was located. Included was Brett waving from the third floor, saying "Hi." What a fun—and safe—way to get into the relationship with the therapist!

—*Mary Ring*

SHAWN, 8

Shawn came into the room unwillingly, to say the least. He had been having a tantrum in the classroom, kicking, throwing chairs around, and stomping on the floor. He had been given the option of settling down, going to the principal's office, or going with the counselor. Shawn reluctantly chose to go with me. As I walked him to my room, Shawn continued his outward display of anger. When we walked into my room, I said to Shawn, "In here you can do many of the things you want." It didn't appear that he had heard a word I said. With a frown on his face and angry squinting of his eyes at me, Shawn forcefully plopped down on the rocking chair. I reflected as much of the outward and inner feelings that I saw and felt in relationship with this child. Shawn turned away from me as if really bothered by my talking, continuing to rock the chair forcefully and occasionally turning only enough so that I could see his contorted little face. I was beginning to feel a bit impatient with myself as I wondered how else I could let this child know that I accepted him unconditionally. Then, as I truly looked at this child, I saw more than just anger; there was a great deal of pain and hurt going on within this silent person.

Shawn finally turned around, sat straight up in the chair, and asked, "Did you say I could do *anything* I wanted in here?" I then responded, "Shawn, in here you can do *many* of the things you want." With a great big smile on his face, Shawn slowly looked around the room and then walked toward the playdough saying, "I think I'll try this first!" With an even greater smile, I said, "Oh! You decided what you're going to do first!" (All I could hear in my mind at this point was: *It works! It works!*) Communicating true acceptance to the child is the first step in allowing the process to flow!   —*Layla Quiroz*

RYAN, 3

One of my favorite "play therapy" experiences was when I was practicing my newfound skills at home, especially letting the kids take responsibility and do things on their own. "That's something you can do" and "You can decide that" were used pretty constantly one particular night. Later in the evening, I asked my son Ryan to bring me a diaper for my 1-year-old. His response was, "Mommy, that's something you can do." (At least he was listening!)

—*Cindy Brownlow*

JILL, 6

Therapist: "I see that you have bangs!"
Jill: "The lady put my bangs on."

—*Doris Omdahl*

SARINA, 5

She entered the playroom for the first time appearing scared and alone, holding both hands to her face and crying. Sarina slowly made her way around the room, finally sitting with her back to me across the room. Looking in the kitchen cabinets, she pulled the doors closely to her side so as not to let me see what she was doing. All the while I kept tracking, looking for every possible movement and reaction to my words. This went on for about 30 minutes until, all of a sudden, Sarina turned and went to the sandbox, now facing me with a smile. By the time the session was over, Sarina was standing at the desk next to me, and when I noted that our time was up, she shook her head "no" and smiled. This reminded me of how amazing the process is and how sacred the relationship is—to the child and to me.

—*Tom Stevens*

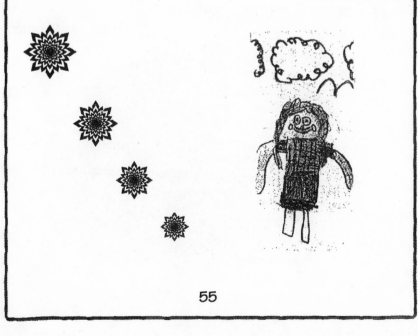

LARA, 5

A frustrated teacher standing in the hall with crying Lara asked if I would *please* see if I could help. After a few minutes of my tracking Lara in the playroom, she ran over and hugged my neck. She then explored the room and talked quite freely. In fact, she announced that she would just stay in the playroom with me for the rest of the day *and* that she cries to get to do the things she wants to do.

The five-minute notice came and then time to go. Lara insisted that she would stay or would cry to have her way. I stuck to the limit, stating that I knew she would really like to stay, but our time in the playroom was up. I dreaded opening the door just knowing that again, Lara would cry loudly, and, consequently, the teacher and other school personnel would think that nothing had been accomplished. However, to my great surprise, when I opened the door and once again calmly stated the limit, Lara got up, took my hand, and happily walked back to class. *The lesson, perhaps, is to TRUST THE PROCESS!*

—*Beckie Thorne*

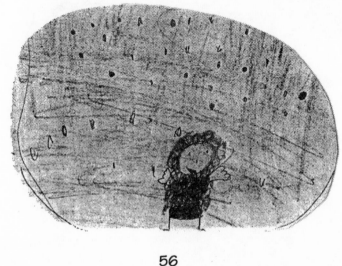

AARON, 8

Aaron swaggered into the playroom with a worldly air. "I've been in therapy before," he announced. "I made up stories to tell, and he treated me for things that weren't even wrong."

Aaron's demeanor softened as he surveyed the playroom. He wondered aloud, "Do I tell you my problems now?" When told *he* could choose, Aaron began to explore this new environment. As the session ended, he revealed that he came with a story all prepared to tell me but I didn't ask questions; besides, he felt too good to tell me a lie. "I think this may be okay," he sighed with some measure of relief. (I think so, too, Aaron!)

—*Barbara Bryant*

BRYAN, 6

Bryan was brought to play therapy because he was "peeing" all over the house. This behavior stopped after five sessions of play therapy and some suggestions for the parents to use at home. However, Bryan's sister picked up where Bryan had left off—"peeing" all over the house. I decided to do sibling play therapy because the bond seemed so tight between the two. One day when we went to the playroom, I offhandedly asked, "Well, how did it go this week?" Bryan puffed up his chest and said, "Me and my sister didn't pee any way at all this week!"

—*Carolyn Adams*

HUNTER, 6

Hunter was experiencing severe separation anxiety. For three sessions, he entered the playroom, asked me what he should do, and then sat at the farthest point from me, back to me, drawing on a piece of paper, never making a sound. In the third session, when I announced that we had five minutes left, Hunter turned around and looked at me. Without hesitation, he slapped his hands on his face with just his nose sticking out and yelled: "Someone please help me open the elevator door!" Then he lowered his hands and started making funny faces at me, never saying another word. I just started laughing, and he did, too! This was a great day for Hunter and me—the breakthrough we needed!! It was downhill from there on.

—*Phyllis Butsch*

EVAN, 5

Evan was busy playing with various toys. After carefully arranging the army men, he said to me, "I have an army truck that these army men need. It's awesome. I guess I'll bring it to the playroom next time." I replied, "Sounds like the army truck is special to you." He looked at me for a second and said, "No, *this playroom is special*, but these guys *need* a truck or they're going to get shot."

—*Debbie Killough*

RICKIE, 5

Rickie, a local recruit for my filial therapy training workshop, was told he was there to help the adults learn how to play with children. Going home, he said to his mother, "They seem kinda big to not know how to play."

—Emily Oe

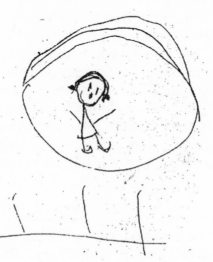

BRENDA

Observing myself on videotape is very helpful. Quickly, I can see my strengths and limitations in facilitating the play therapy process. Observing "pictures" of myself on tape is worth *1,000* words!

—Brenda Horton

NANCY, 7

Nancy joined our play therapy group several months after it had begun. She was a rather serious youngster who was slow to warm up to the group and co-therapists. She often moved about the playroom with a scowl on her face and spoke in a somewhat deep and usually gruff voice which was in sharp contrast to her cute "little girl" appearance.

At about the same time that Nancy was becoming more spontaneous and interactive, I announced to the group that I would be missing the next two sessions, but would return. I took time to explain that I would be traveling to a foreign country across the ocean where people speak a different language—and concluded by saying that I would miss everyone. With a scowl returning to her face and in an emphatic voice, Nancy quickly dismissed my explanation by stating, "Well, then, just don't go!" End of subject!

—*Mary Helen Neal-Craft*

DARREN, 5

Darren had a diagnosis of possible ADD. During the initial sessions, he would play by himself, only involving me to lock me in handcuffs. However, in the middle of the third session, Darren donned a "Lone Ranger" mask, briefly looked at himself in the mirror, and smiled. I responded, "You like how you look in that." Darren then walked directly toward me, slowing as he got closer, and maintaining direct eye contact. He continued until he pressed his forehead against mine, staring into my eyes. He held this position for several seconds, then moved away with a smile. Although I realized that very special contact was allowed with the safety of the mask, I responded, "You really like how you feel wearing that." Darren wore the mask for the remainder of the session, and continued to involve me in more of his play.

—*Donald (Mac) McGuire*

MOLLY, 4

As a beginning play therapist, I was surprised to find out that I could keep my sense of calmness when a child decided to invade my personal space. Molly put every aggressive animal she could find right in my face and made each one "bite" my nose. Not much later, she put a hat on my head. It occurred to me that I could respond with rejection in order to maintain my dignity or I could build my relationship with Molly in the way she needed at the time. I chose to go with the hat and swallow my pride in order to build a stronger relationship with the child. This type of behavior was surprising to me because it was atypical of me to allow others to invade my personal space without having invited them into it. This was the moment in which I realized I could place the child's needs in front of my own as long as I could take care of myself in the process.

—*Charlie Junkin*

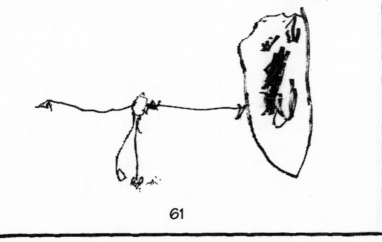

Antonio was processing his father's offenses and his mother's frequenting of night clubs. He created a police car by placing a chair next to the table but facing the easel. A plastic basket of items was pulled to the edge of the table; then, a tear-apart doll was handcuffed to the basket to be taken to the police station. A plastic cucumber and a circular sand sifter served as gear shift and steering wheel. As Antonio started the journey in the police car, he decided that a road was needed.

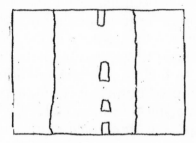

The road being traveled on to the police station.

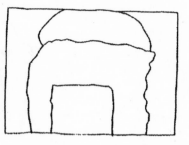

The police station
(painted during the time traveling there).

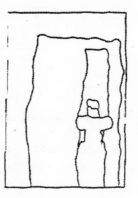

The policeman at the desk as seen through the door.

The policeman at the desk close up.

Antonio and the policeman decided that the tear-apart man was to be thrown into jail. As he removed the handcuffs and threw the man "into jail," Antonio informed the man that he would be back later for a discussion after he had taken care of an emergency. The policeman then ordered Antonio (driver of the police car) to go to the Club and "take care of" the people out there.

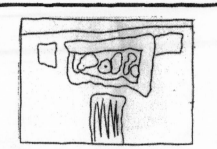

The Club.

Antonio got out of the police car, took the machine guns in the playroom, and gunned down everybody inside the Club.

—*Mary Ring*

DEANA, 4

With a history of sexual molestation by several people as well as family relocation with temporary separation from Dad, Deana was very hesitant in the playroom. She quietly sat on a chair until the therapist noted: "You seem very sad." Then, soft crying began until it escalated to stronger and stronger sobbing followed many times by "I want my Mommy." Upon seeing her mother, Deana immediately said, "I don't want to go with her again; she hurt me." In response to her mother's questioning, Deana replied, "She hurt my heart." How awesome to know how much I touched her pain with just one little, caring observation!

—*Anonymous*

GREG, 8

When I was a field practicum student, the time to close sessions with clients had arrived. Greg had been a client for a short time, and I was apprehensive about closure—knowing that there were issues far from resolved. As usual, Greg asked me what he should do; as usual, I responded with empowering statements and enjoyed the glow on his face as he discovered untapped potential. Greg decided that he wanted to make a butterfly, pausing only to ask which color he should use next. Again, my responses were ones of empowerment, and Greg finished painting his butterfly. A look of satisfaction was followed by concentrated cutting out of the butterfly. When the session ended, Greg frowned and groaned, placed the butterfly on the table, and walked out. Although time for closure had come too soon for me, Greg was ready to spread his wings and fly—and he left me with wings of my own in the form of a butterfly.

—*Cindy Hammonds*

DEAN, 7

Dean started the session with aggressive play—using soldiers, guns, other weapons. He went to the wooden pegs and pounded very hard with wide swings.

> "It feels like I'm pounding the devil. Take this (POUND)! Take that (POUND)! I hate the devil!"

Dean got the devil puppet and threw it on the floor, stabbing it repeatedly with small knives and a large sword. He then threw darts for a while (a skill he had mastered).

Then, Dean put on angel wings and a halo, stating: "I'm a little angel." Still wearing the angel gear, he spread out the floor checker game. "Have you ever seen an angel playing checkers? Well, I *am* one." (It seemed to him a funny picture—he, Dean, an angel—sitting on the floor playing checkers.)

—*Judi Gilbert*

TYLER, 5

After five sessions, there was a drastic change in Tyler's playroom behavior. Instead of exploring and involving me in his play, Tyler "destroyed" the playroom. He took everything off the shelves, knocked over the table and chairs, and moved the kitchen set across the room. *Tyler* left the playroom in a *huff*. Needless to say, I left the playroom a little *shocked*.

Tyler did the same the next session. As I suspected would happen, he did the same the next session, also. However, when he was through before the time was up, Tyler surveyed the chaos, smiled, and said, "Now, I can rest." Tyler never made a mess after that.

—*Leigh McRae*

MEGAN, 5

While taking my first play therapy class, I often practiced my responses on my daughter, Megan. Now, two years later, when I use too much "therapeutic" language, Megan rolls her eyes and sighs, "Mom, you're talking funny again!" Perhaps she thinks that I have some intermittent speech disease!

—*Phyllis Butsch*

DENISE, 10

After 18 months of therapy, very physically mature Denise openly talked about her abuse. At the end of the session, Denise suddenly turned and said, "Wait." Then, she picked up the baby bottle and began sucking as hard and fast as she could. Denise looked at me with a sigh, took off the nipple and lid, guzzled the water. "There," she said with a satisfied grin and wet with dripping water, "I'm ready to go."

—*Carolyn Adams*

SARA, 5

Sara enjoyed her time in the playroom. Each session, she removed her shoes and slid her little feet deep into the sand, turning to me with a big smile, sharing her pleasure with me.

After session six, Sara missed two sessions while on vacation with her family. The first session after her return began as usual. She played in the sandbox for a while, then decided to play with the musical instruments. As Sara walked to the shelf, she turned to me suddenly and said, "I missed you." What an inspiration those three little words were for me and how they plucked my heart of hearts!

—*Peggy Vaughn–Foerster*

TAYLOR, 4

Over a period of four months, Taylor became very agitated whenever it was time to leave our sessions. One day, she looked up from her sandplay after being reminded that it was time to leave and said, "Well, do you mind?! I'm working!"

—*Robin Lee*

TREVOR, 6

This was the second year Trevor was in play therapy, and his sudden tantrums, outbursts, and stubborn shutdowns were less frequent in the classroom. Although Trevor usually circled the playroom, occasionally stopping to play with one thing or another, he always settled in at the easel.

Not being proficient in art interpretation, I was still pleased when Trevor painted a picture of what appeared to be an apple tree with the usual brown trunk, green leaves, and red dots for apples—and a yellow "sun" circle in the top left corner. Then, he made a brown square and a triangle on top of a brown house, finishing it off with a large, red blob in the center. There were no windows or doors. Over the house, Trevor painted a large, black oval smear on which he put four yellow crosses. I was bewildered and distressed. I *rarely* ask for interpretations, but upon leaving, I could not help myself, so I said, "Trevor, tell me about your picture." Trevor began with the apple tree and the bright sun that the apples need for growing. (Good, I was on track.) The house was very warm because it had a big fireplace in the center of it, and last night, they had looked at the bright, sparkly stars. It was fun!

Weeks later, Trevor painted four black blobs spread out across the paper with two stick figures near the center in line with each other and close by two of the black blobs. He painted the top of the paper all black with a large yellow circle in the top corner. He painted a red blob near one stick figure and smeared it almost touching the second figure and on into the black part. I will leave it up to you to share in the thoughts I was experiencing! I am a slow learner, so, once again, I could not help saying, "Trevor, tell me about your picture." He appeared quite excited and proud of it.Trevor talked about his baseball game the night before, how his friend had hit a home run, and winning!

—*Vicky Mahaffey*

70

TOM

....

Who would have ever thought that letting the child have control is the key to getting things done! When I think about play therapy, I immediately think about feelings. It is not the way I do play therapy that determines how effective I am. It is the way I feel about it and care about it and dedicate myself to it that is most important. When I am dedicating myself to play therapy, I am also dedicating myself to children. Play therapy is not my way of doing it; rather, it is the child's way.

—*Tom Stevens*

KYRA, 36

In an *adult* group play therapy session, Kyra stated that she was so happy playing with another group member because she was "playing rather than trying to play at playing." She realized that as a child, she had always played "seriously" and usually by herself, never feeling accepted, safe, or free enough to be spontaneous in play.

—*Lois Hansen*

MARY

As I struggled to learn the appropriate responses in the playroom, I had the most difficulty giving up a directive role. I knew I was making headway when I got in the car one day with my husband who was driving. When he asked for directions, I said, "You get to decide."

—*Mary Ring*

CANDEE, 4

For our home-based therapy, Candee and I were having our session under a tree in her front yard. She decided to put my rather short hair in pigtails all over my head. Next, she had me put on the bright blue high-heeled shoes and selected a purse for each of us.

Candee: "Okay, it's time to go to church. You carry the baby. I'm driving; you ride in the back with the baby."

By this time, we were at the end of the driveway on a busy corner with a 4-way stop.

Candee: "Okay. Now, clap your hands the way I do. March!" Now, I'm clapping, carrying a baby and a purse, while attempting to march in an oversized pair of high heels.

Candee: "No, Miss Susan. Like this!" She demonstrated how I was to swing my hips, lower my head just a little, raise my knees up and down, and clap, adding, "Sing, Miss Susan, sing!"

Imagine a small child and a middle–aged woman (bright blue shoes, purse, baby doll in arms, hair in pigtails) on a busy corner marching around and around the grandmother's car, singing very loudly off-key. We altered the flow of traffic in that area of town!

After the session, Candee ran inside: "Grandma, Grandma! Miss Susan and I went to church." Such a big smile!!

—*Susan Corley*

LANA, 4

During the 25 minutes that Lana stood next to me without moving, I realized that I was okay and so was she. I just needed to track her standing there. Once I relaxed, it was easier than I had thought. I just began to look at every little thing about her—just to be *with* her *in the moment.*

—*Marianne Hampton*

TROY, 5

In the waiting room, a mother was overheard teaching 5-year-old Troy to count on the abacus. Finally, Troy frustratedly reprimanded his mother: "Mom, let me think for myself!"

—*Anonymous*

LEON, 10

As an outpatient therapist in a school setting with children who come from some very troubling circumstances, I see many children who have already internalized a shattered and hostile view of the world by the time I see them. However, there is a wonderful sense of the absurd that a therapist can bring to a child through the medium of play. On more than one occasion, this magical breaking of respected boundaries has proven an effective force for me in joining with a young client.

One day, I was called by the classroom teacher because Leon had been taken to the time-out room after being verbally abusive to a teacher. Although I had had only two brief encounters with him prior to this outburst, I had quickly determined that one of his strengths and probably his best coping mechanism was a sense of humor that surfaced only fleetingly.

As I entered the time-out room, I saw Leon curled up on the punching bag in a fetal position with his T-shirt pulled over his face. I sat next to him for several minutes shaping a small figure from the ball of modeling clay that I often carry with me on such occasions. I opened my intuition to the circumstances and thought, "If I were this child, what would offer me comfort?" Then, I shaped a shield for the small clay man to hold. Once this was accomplished, I thought, "Now, how can I make contact with this child in a nonthreatening manner?" I shaped a feather out of clay for the "man" to hold in his other hand. I gently "walked" the clay man over to Leon with his shirt pulled over his face and lightly touched him on his arm with the "feather." Then, feigning fear, the clay man quickly retreated and held up his "shield." The second and third foray to touch Leon's arm lightly produced the subtlest of cues that he was becoming aware that something magically absurd was behind the light, slightly greasy touch on his arm. He lowered the neckline of his T-shirt to peek out. Quickly, the "man" retreated, holding up his shield and saying "Oo, oo, oo" in a nervous, tense manner. When Leon snorted and pulled his shirt back over his eyes, the clay man advanced to tickle the exposed arm one more time. With only two more advances and nervous retreats, Leon laughed and sat up. With all the admiration that a street-wise 10-year-old could muster, he said, "You're weird, lady." (I accepted the compliment graciously!) Then, we talked about how scared the clay man was of Leon because of his menacingly large size and about how the man was brave enough to take action anyway.

Of course, the metaphor of the tiny clay man against the enormously large child paralleled the enormity of Leon's daily challenges. Leon leaned over and scooped up the little clay figure, asking, "Can we save this guy?" This powerful and swift joining was a moment where the transforming nature of art, play, and two lives intersected to produce magic. It was a short step from this moment to Leon's accepting responsibility for his inappropriate behavior which had led to his placement in the time-out room. The continuing work with this child, who had been described as "hostile and defensive," flowed easily from this initial therapeutic encounter. Leon began to identify with the clay "warrior" equipped with a feather rather than a sword.

—*Luanne Baker*

KYLE, 8

For six months, Kyle, an adopted child, had been "throwing away" his past issues in a trashbag, a trashcan, or the sandbox. During the 32nd session, he sequentially threw away in the trashcan selected objects "to burn," objects he had broken (like the lid of a toy pan), and objects to just throw away. Toward the end of the session, Kyle wrote his name and mine on separate strips of paper towel and placed them in the trashcan for a "drawing." He purposely drew his own name and declared himself the winner of the trashcan, proudly taping his name to the edge of his prized possession. Then Kyle taped my name to the other side of the trashcan, stating, "We can share this trashcan together." How precious it was for this child to officially share with me this trashcan of such value to him and to the therapeutic process when, in reality, he had been sharing it with me for 32 sessions!

—*Theresa Fusaro*

DEBBIE

I had been trying very hard to use my play therapy communication skills at home and recently had the opportunity to babysit with three nephews and a niece. For the third time, I encouraged the two 3-year-olds to get into their chairs. The 5-year-old commented, "Ooh, that's an angry voice." My reply was, "It was? I didn't intend for it to be." He was certain to let me know how he experienced it when he said, "Well, kids think it is."

—*Debbie McDowell*

TOMMY

As a beginning play therapist, I have discovered that I cannot bear to set limits. I admit that my two clients are complete angels, but I just can't see myself setting limits. Once I am in the playroom with either child, I feel as though the child can do no wrong. I see each of the child's actions as something the child really wants to do, so who am I to stop it? This is the child's time—right? However, I do know when the time comes, I *will* be able to set limits *and* feel good about it because, even then, I will be inspired by the play of children.

—*Tommy Wilbeck*

LACEY, 6

During a school group play therapy session of 6-and 7-year-olds (2 girls, 1 boy), Lacey asked, "Ms. Mahaffey, how come you always know what we're feeling?" Bingo! I had mastered reflection, at least in that session!

—*Vicky Mahaffey*

DALE, 5

Whenever Dale and I were in a play therapy session together, I allowed him to tap into a very intimidated and scared 3-year-old little girl lurking inside me. My defenses shot up every time as Dale pounded around the room telling me to "stop talking!," having the dinosaurs bite me, and throwing balls all around me. At first, I fought the little Kimberly, trying to stuff her down; she cried and was even more scared. Finally, going into the playroom by myself, I allowed her to play. I tracked her silently. As I left the playroom, I decided to allow that scared little girl out once a week for an hour, but, in therapy with Dale, she was protected and loved by the adult Kimberly. The next session with Dale, I calmly set limits; counter-transference never again occurred and Dale never again asked me to stop talking.

—*Kimberly Dillon*

WILLIAM, 5

This was William's final session. His presenting problem behaviors had disappeared or diminished—clingy, whiny, demanding behavior with his mother; expressing the belief that he would "be okay if Mother dies and she goes to heaven"; babyish language; soliciting others to do tasks that he could do. However, I did not believe William and I ever had formed a therapeutic relationship that was significant to him. Throughout the 20 sessions, he repeatedly had asked, "Is this the last time I have to come here?" or had said, "I don't want to go today" or, more directly, "I am not going to see Dr. Perry today." William was all grins when I talked with him about ending our special time together.

Prior to this final play session, William's mother attempted to get him to tell me about a bad dream he had had the previous night. He refused, but asked his mother to tell me. I intervened with, "That's okay. You can tell me the dream when you decide you want to tell me." It was all William could do to wait until we got into the playroom. Barely had I closed the door when William blurted out, "It was so quiet and weird. There were these green eyes. I couldn't see any face, but I heard this voice saying, 'Follow me.'" William used a deep, ghostlike voice. He then told how he had gone to seek safety with his sister and finally returned to his own bed. However, he kept thinking about those green eyes and the scary voice saying "Follow me."

I suggested that William show me what the eyes looked like by drawing them on a piece of paper. He eventually covered a piece of brown construction paper with large green eyes, talking about how spooky the eyes looked, what they might see, and how even when he closed his eyes, he could still see them.

I wondered aloud how William might get rid of those scary-looking green eyes, and we took turns suggesting means of destruction. William chose to "cut them up." However, as he began to cut, rather than cutting them *up*, he cut them *out*. After cutting out two, he announced, "They are now green eggs." After cutting out two more, he proposed a game of hide-and-seek, using the cut-out green eggs. So, we took turns hiding and finding the green eggs with William giving me many clues to help me find the eggs he had hidden.

When William wearied of the game, he decided we would play doctor, with William as doctor and me as patient. (Fantasy play involving me in the story was not his usual play therapy behavior.) Using the toy phone, William directed me to call and make an appointment to come in and see him. After checking me with the doctor's kit instruments, he gave me a shot, some medicine, and a cup of water, and told me to go home. As he also directed me, I called him again for another appointment. Following my check-up this time, William informed me he would be going on a 10-month vacation!

So, William and I parted with his play session a wonderful example of how children use play so expertly to handle their fears (e.g., changing scary green eyes into delightful green hiding eggs). The termination issue also was handled so adeptly through play as he treated and "cured" me, and then gave both of us a "vacation" from our special time. Also, again, I was reminded that my perception of the therapeutic relationship as less than ideal does not mean that it carries little significance for the child!

—*Lessie Perry*

RICHARD, 6

Recently, I had an urgent call from a woman whose fiancé had just been killed by a drunk driver in a car accident. She began grief counseling with me. Several weeks into therapy, she came eager to share something with me, with the first smile I had seen on her saddened face and the first hint of hope in her voice! Here is what she related:

> Last night I felt so drained and depressed that I just lay down on my sofa after feeding the kids. Soon, Richard sat down beside me and said, "Mommy, do you remember that lady you took me to play with after you and Daddy got divorced? Maybe *you* should go play with her now."

(Richard is now 6 years old and just a year ago had been in play therapy with me for six months.)

—*Faye Wedell*

MR. CRANSTON, 93

In the middle of various activities, Mr. Cranston took great delight in looking at me and saying, "You are better than punch."

—*Beverly Lilie*

MARY

The most difficult thing for me to do as a play therapist is not to label objects unless the child does so first. I feel redundant calling everything "this" or "that." I become so aware of what not to do that I begin to stumble over my own words in mid-sentence. Then the sentence has no chance of making sense, or at least I don't think so. However, I guess *that's* what happens when you do something like *this*!

—*Mary Sullivan*

JANET

Eager to embark on my new career as an elementary school counselor, I began to shop for my playroom supplies. Budgets being what they are, I went to my favorite local K-Mart. With limited space and the prompting of my professor, I decided to use a litterbox for my sand-tray. Much distressed at being unable to locate the item, I sought out a store clerk and asked for the litterboxes. She asked, "For a cat?" I replied, "No, it's for children." Reading her nonverbals, I thought it best to explain, "I use it at school." In dismay, I realized there was no turning back, so I simply smiled and left.

—*Janet Berner*

PHILIP, 3

Philip was ready to leave the playroom before his time was up. He first began testing the limits by telling me that he wanted to go outside and play. I acknowledged his feelings and request, but that wasn't enough for Philip because he tried to pull me out of the chair to go outside. When I still didn't get up to go outside with him, Philip opened and closed the door, repeating his request to go outside and play. I allowed him to verbalize his need, and stated that he really wanted to go outside but his time in the playroom was not over. With three minutes left,  Philip opened the door and took a step into the hallway. He came back in when the limit was stated again and taught me that children will follow limits even though they may be testing them.

—*Jennifer Rodes*

SHERRY

I am amazed at how much I really like children! I have always suspected this, but never knew how to explore it further. Everyone else always seemed to know how to talk to children, and I didn't. I would just kind of stare, trying to make a connection by being interested, making faces, or acting silly. When the children were unhappy, I would feel sad and be unable to show that I cared. Eventually, I would become frustrated and controlling because I just didn't know what to do. *NOW*, I am *learning* what to do within this play therapy world.

—*Sherry Jones*

84

THE LITTLE ONE

The Little One
goes about the business
of recreating his world
as he perceives it.

As I watch, I revel
in the wisdom and
accuracy that most
of us have missed.

He sees his life and
those who take part.
He wonders how they
overlook the business
he is in,
Mistaking it for unimportant.

—*Sherri Marshall Briggs*

From: <u>APT Newsletter</u>, 10(3), 1991.

FELICIA

When I was role playing in my initial play therapy course, another student shot the dart gun at me. I let out a slight yelp and jumped out of my "therapist's" chair. I couldn't keep from flinching every time he shot near me. This taught me that I needed to work on my own issue with guns. So, I visited my relatives and let my nephews and nieces practice shooting *toward* me over and over, which they loved to do (within limits, of course!).

—*Felicia Pratscher*

KENT, 6

During a puppet play interaction, Kent is reflecting on the events of his day. Says Kent (in the role of the puppet): "My friend told me that my girlfriend wanted to kiss me."

Therapist (in the role of the other puppet): "How did that make you feel?"

Kent: "It made me feel like I'm never going to eat pizza again."

JOYCE, 6

I do group play therapy with Joyce and her younger brother. Often, Joyce seems very frustrated as she asks, "Why do you always talk that way?" One day, she surprised me at the end of a session when she resisted leaving the playroom and said, "I wish I could stay here forever and never have any problems. I love it here."

—*Sherrie Mullen*

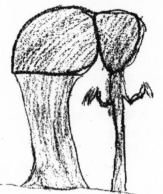

JESSICA, 5

Jessica made the phone ring and then answered it. She pretended to listen to the caller and then responded, "I can't talk right now; I'm in play therapy!"

—*Linda Homeyer*

VICTORIA

I keep learning how much I *LOVE* play therapy!

—*Victoria Valz*

JAY, 9

Jay and I were on an outdoor outing. As a child who has had to work with social services and community mental health liaisons far too much, Jay is used to people telling him what to do. On this particular occasion, we were at the bottom of a rock ledge. Once the person has climbed to the top of the ledge, he can look over a cliff and into a large pond below.

Most people would have prevented Jay from climbing to the top. He does not consider his personal safety most of the time in other situations, and this would have been a problem for most other liaisons. When Jay asked me if I thought the climb was too dangerous, I replied, "That's something you can decide."

The sense of accomplishment was overwhelming. When Jay reached the top, his face was beaming. "Look!" he exclaimed. "I did it!" I converted to child-centered philosophy right then and there.

—James von Grabow

JORDY, 6

As Jordy approached the playroom door, he looked at me and said, "This is going to be good!" He walked in and looked around as he stood in the middle of the floor. Eyes focused on the shelves, he stated emphatically, "This is *too* good." For five minutes, he just stood looking around and repeating, "I just don't know what I want to do." Finally, Jordy stated, "I'm going to put on my thinking hat and my *good* 'looking' hat." Pretending to put on the hat, he pointed his finger, and confidently said, "Now, I know what I'm going to do."

—*Stephanie Stevens*

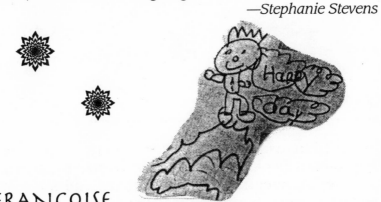

FRANÇOISE

Working with each individual child helps me get in touch with my inner child and realize how precious she is. Just as she wanted to be heard and noticed long ago, so does every little one with whom I come in contact. Over and over, I experience such deep reverence for the "sparkling" little children and awe for the miracle awakenings germinating and beginning to sprout right in front of my eyes.

—*Françoise Cisneros*

KEITH, 6

As Keith and I entered the playroom, I brought up the fact that it had been two weeks since we had a session. The first absence, I explained, was due to spring break, but the second, however, was because I was sick.

"I knew you weren't going to come," said Keith.

"Oh, so you knew I wasn't coming," I reflected.

"That's right," said Keith emphatically, "*God* told me."

—*Kimberly Dillon*

BERNA, 5

I decided to rearrange my office to incorporate play therapy in my school setting. I received favorable comments on the changes from both teachers and students. However, Berna's reaction was the most precious. She opened the door and exclaimed, "Barbieland!"

—*Layla Quiroz*

LAURIE, 3

Forehead furrowed, Laurie commented, "You don't have any bangs on your head," and ran her hand across her own forehead. I noted, "You noticed that I don't have much hair up there. Seems like you've been looking at me a bit." Adamantly, Laurie replied, "I've been looking at you *a lot*!"

—*Tom Stevens*

DEVON, 7

My work is mainly with children adjusting to their parents' divorce. I often have a father come into the session as an observer—of course with the child's permission. Recently, Devon was playing and talking about how sad he gets at bedtime when his father is not there. He also talked about his fears of sleeping upstairs by himself. I said, "Seems like you don't have ways to help yourself feel safe." He thought a minute and then said, "Well, I sing 'Jesus Loves Me.'" There were tears in his father's eyes.

—*Jeanette Mallory*

ZOE, 4

Zoe wasn't at all sure she wanted to be in this play therapy room with me. Her initial session had just begun and she stood stiffly, as if glued to the floor, holding a small rubber ball. One finger continued to rub back and forth over the sticky residue left from the price tag. Zoe's eyes, opened wide, continued to stare at me like a startled deer caught in the headlights of a car. I reflected to her that I knew it was "sometimes scary to be in here for the first time." I assured her that she "could play with the toys in lots of the ways she'd like to" and that, in here, she "could decide to play or just stand right there." After I continued to reflect for 15 long, long minutes, Zoe suddenly dropped the ball, walked purposefully toward the puppets, and tossed a comment over her shoulder as she went: "I've decided not to be scared anymore."

—*Linda Homeyer*

JAMIE, 7

Quite descriptively portraying a teacher frequently raising her voice, Jamie paused in the middle of writing a child's name on the board for punishment. "No, I'm going to call your mother." Ring, ring, ring. "Hello, Mrs. Smith. No, I'm calling about something *good* your daughter did. Your daughter, she's . . . she's . . . she's a *CHAMPION*! Okay, I'll call you again someday when she does something else."

—*Anonymous*

MARK, 3; MARANDA, 7

A client's mother described her children's behavior after play therapy sessions: "They're absolutely famished and exhausted after a session. It's almost like they've been at swim practice. I'm telling you that play therapy is work; they're *really* working hard in there!"

—*Sherrie Mullen*

JENNIFER

Entering the world of a child through play therapy is truly an enlightening experience. Many people tend to think that children must be told what to do and when to do it. I have never truly believed in this idea, and play therapy gives me the opportunity to empower children in making their own decisions. Certainly, children are our world's greatest resources, and play therapy allows them to develop their own resources. I encourage all counselors to use play therapy to *truly* help children.

—*Jennifer Rodes*

LANIKA, 4

With her artwork and shoes bundled in her arms, Lanika approached the waiting room door at the end of her session. She looked up at me, stared at the doorknob, and then looked back at me as if to say, "Open the door." After a smile and pause, I waited with Lanika at the door. She let out a sigh, placed her shoes between her legs, turned the doorknob, grabbed her shoes, and stated, "I know; that's something I can do!" and rolled her eyes as she walked out the door.

—*Jill Johnson*

LARRY, 7

Larry: "When I grow up, I'm going to work at McDonald's."
Therapist: "So, you know what you want to do."
Larry: "No . . . I'm going to be the manager. Then, you can come in and have everything free!"

—*Anonymous*

KRISTIN, 8

In the transition process from play therapy with me to the school psychologist, I went to the school to have one last lunch with Kristin. She greeted me with a big smile and immediate information: "I had play therapy with Miss Judy. She is just like you. She [Miss Judy] said that in here I could decide. I told her that's what Susan says; Miss Judy's just like you!"

—*Susan Corley*

KELLY, 6

The intake read that Kelly was considered a "low-functioning, learning-disabled, possibly brain-damaged child" with additional speculation of sexual abuse in a foster home. In the midst of Kelly's tantrums, she portrayed a "mean man." She swore viciously; simple time-out for small infractions became a "jail"; she punished herself unmercifully. She sang "Oh, Baby, Baby" in a provocative, low voice with hips gyrating and other clues as to the nature of the "mean man."

In the playroom, Kelly began slowly to separate herself from the "mean man." We played "Call the sheriff and arrest this guy" hundreds of times. During the arrest, the male doll figure was led away, arms handcuffed behind his back. However, he always returned to scare the little girl figure. Sometimes he tied her to the bed; sometimes he urged her to "Come here, baby; gimme a kiss"; sometimes he screamed "Shut up; shut up!" when the little girl cried.

Even though Kelly became more free and her work and play became lighter and more positive in her daily life, the "mean man" remained an important part of Kelly's play therapy experience for at least part of each session.

After many, many sessions, Kelly put the "mean man" in the dollhouse "time-out bed" for saying some "really bad words." She was hoping he would stay there for a while so she could have some fun in the sandtable. However, he kept escaping, and she just couldn't completely relax. Kelly tried tying him into the bed "like he did to me" (one of her few direct verbalizations about the abuse), but he broke loose.

I asked, "Would tape keep him in?" She put pieces of tape on his arms and legs to keep him in bed and across his mouth to keep him from swearing, but again he got away. She had to call the sheriff to help her put him back in the time-out bed. From there, Kelly used various taping schemes and *MUCH*, *MUCH* tape to restrain the "mean man" and to keep him from swearing—wrapping and wrapping with  delight, chuckling, shrieking with laughter, her eyes wide, her face flushed pink with the seeming abandonment of all propriety and sanity. Kelly had found a physical and external way to rid herself of the "mean man" who had controlled her inner life so completely.

Kelly's play during the next few months progressed to joyous parades through the sand as well as beautiful farms with the animals and people all happily living together without fear. Rowdy, the spike-backed little dinosaur, led the way, and every session with Kelly and Rowdy became a birthday party and Christmas all in one. Many decorated sandpies and cakes were delivered to my door, and invitations to tea parties came in with each day's mail.

Those were moments to treasure, precious moments of integration, psychosexual delineation, *a celebration of the human spirit*—never to be totally reproduced in print or verbally for anyone else. As the old saying goes, "You had to be there."

—*Carol Whited*

VICKY

School counselors often are put in compromising positions of "Duty" where we are expected to "control" children. Thank goodness for play therapy terms to keep me in good standing with the students and feeling good about my title of "Counselor" (e.g., "Running is not for the halls." "Yelling is not for the cafeteria; you can choose to talk quietly or whisper." "Fighting/Cussing is not for school." "Food is for eating or keeping on your tray." "S/he is not for calling names."). Usually, alternatives were not required because my reminders were enough. Amazingly, I began to hear some teachers begin to use the terminology, instead of "Don't," "Can't," or "Shouldn't!"

—*Vicky Mahaffey*

SORI, 4

Sori was referred for play therapy after extensive testing and conflicting diagnoses ranging from autism to schizophrenia. During her first session, she went to one corner of the playroom. After a *long* pause, Sori began to take the toys off the shelves and throw them in the middle of the floor. She took apart everything that could come apart, including taking all the clothes off the dolls. She continued around the room until *every* toy was in the middle of the floor. Finally, Sori surveyed the items, sat in the middle of them, cupped her head in her hands, and sighed heavily. She sat for several minutes looking content, as if to say: "Finally, I have stopped the chaos— if only for a moment."

—*Debbie Killough*

LAKEITHA, 5

"Street-smart" Lakeitha was approaching the end of her 16th play therapy session. She had been referred by Child Protective Services because her parents were "druggies" who habitually binged and neglected her for long periods of time. Her father also battered her mother and physically abused Lakeitha whenever she intervened. Finally, the mother decided to get treatment and to divorce the father.

Weekly, Lakeitha became more empowered as she played out two recurring themes: the role of a wife/mother who stood up to her abusive spouse and protected her children, and the role of a little girl who had an ideal family with an especially loving father. I knew she had reached a measure of resolution when she was playing the role of the mother and blurted out to me, "Kid, which do you love most—me or your daddy? Oh, that's all right, Kid; you can love us both. You don't have to like your daddy to love him, Kid!"

In preparing for termination, I asked Lakeitha just what she liked best about coming to the special playroom. She answered, "Well, it's the only place I get to be the Line Leader every time I come." At first, I didn't catch on; then, I took time to look at the world through *her* eyes and remembered that being the Line Leader in kindergarten is the epitome of prestige and honor. What she was truly saying was, *"In here, I really matter!"*

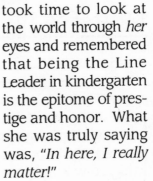

—Faye Wedell

99

JACLYN, 9

Jaclyn insisted, "I'm tired of you talking all the time. I want you to draw a picture instead." Eventually, I asked her what and how she wanted me to draw. Jaclyn replied, "However you want." So, I drew a rainbow of many different colors and wrote my name on one of the color bands. Jaclyn took the drawing and quickly wrote her name on top of the rainbow and said, "Now, you will never be that far away from me again!" One can never underestimate the power of the play therapy relationship and the impact one can have in a child's life.

—Deborah Holzman

RODNEY, 10

Rodney was in a really good mood on this particular evening when he asked me if he could pretend to be a "palm reader." When I agreed, he proceeded to the paint easel with a smirk on his face. Rodney picked up a paint-brush and quickly came over to me. To my surprise, he painted my hand red. With great delight, he said, "You said you wanted your palm 'red'!"

—Pat Ledyard

SHELBY, 3

Shelby was being seen initially because of sexual abuse by her birth mother's boyfriend. However, as her therapy continued, it became clear that her primary therapeutic issue was the court-ordered monthly visits to her maternal grandmother and birth mother. Not only did Shelby not want to visit, but they did not believe her outcry of sexual abuse and often attempted to manipulate her to recant and forced her to verbalize words of affection.

Shelby worked hard to be in control of many things in the play therapy room. She simply wanted to be in control of something in her life. So many people told her what she must do, where she must go, what she must allow to happen to her, and whom she was supposed to love. Therefore, it was a great and wondrous day when, as Shelby was painting at the easel and singing to herself a made-up song

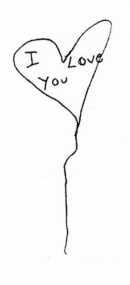

about colors, she addressed me: "Miss Linda?" "Yes, Shelby," I responded. "I love you," Shelby said. *Finally*, she had discovered a safe and permissive place where she was valued simply for being— a place where she could decide whom she loved and when and how she would share it.

Moments like this are the pay-off for all the difficult sessions.

—*Linda Homeyer*

MY DOG JUST HAD KITTENS BUT YOU JUST YELLED

Why is it that you can't hear
what I say?

The computer turned into a
   monster last night when
   you turned out the lights.
It marched around the room eating everything in sight.
When it came close to me, I crawled under my bed.
   But, it ate my brother.
   He screamed and screamed, but you didn't hear.
I woke up shaking all over, wanting to be close to you.
But you said, "Go back to your room. And now!
You woke me up. I have to go to work tomorrow!"

Why can't you hear what I say?
Don't you know I have feelings, too?

Snuggles, my cat, curled close when I was afraid,
   But you yelled, "Get that cat out of the house.
   Look what it did on your floor!"
Snuggles knows when I hurt.
Why don't you?

Why is it that you can't hear what I feel?

At school today, I was teased about the way my hair
   looked.
I felt really angry, and hit him hard.
The teacher was so mad at me.
She took me right to the principal's office.
Never once did she ask me why I was so mad.

Why is it she can't hear what I feel, either?

My brother told me to get out of his way.
He never says anything nice to me.
I hate him!
Why does he make me so angry?

Doesn't anyone care what I feel?

The cops came and took Daddy away when I was only four.
He never listened to me.
He only yelled, "Get away from the front of the TV.
   Can't you see I'm watching the football game?"
Now, he is gone, but I don't care.
I don't like him anyway.

I went to a new place today.
A room full of toys just for me.
"You can do most anything you want to do in here," she said.
She sat in a chair, and watched everything I did.
When I knocked the toys off the shelf, she said, "You
   feel really angry."
When I jumped rope really fast, she said, "You
   seemed pleased about that."
I asked, "Can I play in the sand?" She said, "In here,
   you can decide."

Wow, finally someone does hear
   what I feel!
I wish everyone knew how to
   talk like that!
                    —Pat Ledyard

103

PEDRO, 4

Aggressive behavior almost had warranted Pedro's removal from daycare. One session, he was covering the alligator with sand. Head down, Pedro murmured, "Some alligators are bad. They try to be good, but sometimes they're bad." His struggle was so evident!

—*Judi Gilbert*

ERNIE, 6

Without verbalization, Ernie chose to shoot suction-cup darts at the wall and at targets he created. Watching and reflecting, I was starting to hope for a break in *my* monotony. Finally, Ernie put his guns down for a second and glanced at the dolls and stuffed animals. I inflected my voice and smiled, working hard to offer him *an opportunity*. It almost seemed like Ernie sniffed at the air, turned his nose up, and went back to what he was doing, as if he knew playing with something else was a *therapist's wish* instead of his. Somehow, I think there is some intuition going on. Children sense things with special antennae!

—*James von Grabow*

REBECCA, 9

Rebecca was determined not to stay in the playroom. She kicked, scratched, and yelled, insisting that she did not have to stay. When that behavior was limited, she proceeded to throw everything she could find . . . at me! Definitely, she was *not* out of control! She knew at all times just where she was throwing—in arc positions that landed the items all around me but never on me so as to hurt me.

Many sessions later, Rebecca handcuffed me to the cupboard door, and then walked over to the playroom door. *"I could leave if I want to."* "I guess you're right about that." Coming back and leaning thoughtfully on the cupboard, she asked, *"Do you remember that first time I came in here?"* "Seems like *you're* thinking about that." *"I was really a brat, wasn't I?"* "You don't seem very happy about the way you acted." Even after so many sessions where our relationship seemed so good, she still needed to know if I was holding a grudge! Trust is such a tenuous thing!!

—*Emily Oe*

Week 1

I walk, uncertain, into the room.
I am too scared, and don't know what to do.
I don't feel good being with other girls and boys.
I don't want to play with stupid toys.

I watch the others playing with dolls and paints.
I wish I could join in, but my heart is faint.
I sit in the corner and stay out of the way.
I wish I could leave it for another day.

I don't want to play with others in here.
I feel sick to my stomach because of my fear.
I wish I could leave it for another day.
One little girl asks me to play.

"I don't want to play; just leave me alone."
I feel so stupid, just want to go home.
The others are playing and having some fun.
Why can't I let go; I want to run!

The paint easel is set up and ready
But this little boy's hand isn't steady.
The little boy doesn't want to paint with them.
What if the others make fun of him?

The xylophone sits on its shelf all alone.
I wish I could play it but I don't strike a tone.
I would play if the others would leave.
I would paint flowers and maybe some trees.

There are too many people in the room.
Maybe I could sit in my corner and hum a tune.
My "playmates" seem to be having a good time.
I sit alone in the corner, not sharing my rhymes.
Others are playing with a house of wood.
 I want to smash it—but that isn't "good."

One little girl is reading aloud to friends.
I wish she wouldn't read, playing "pretend."
She seems to be having a whole lot of fun.
I wish I could leave; I wish I could run!

I see others playing with play army guns.
I wish they would leave, so I could have fun.
This room full of toys would be so ideal
If time here alone I could steal.

I would paint flowers and beautiful trees.
It's all inside, a part of me.
I could make music on the xylophone.
I could talk on the play telephone.

I wish I was the only child in the room.
I could play soldier; I could play tunes.
I would build buildings from the big cardboard blocks.
I could build a house with a BIG, BIG lock.

If the others would leave me here all alone,
I could build my castle and be king on my throne.
No one could hurt me, in this world of my own.
No one could tell me "Shut up," or "Go on."

I would pretend I was a child so free.
I could feel like I hadn't sinned, you see?
I would stand tall, be proud of myself.
I wouldn't be like the doll on the shelf.

I could run and jump and play.
I wish I could be alone here, for the whole day.
If I were alone with all the toys
I could be happy being a boy.

Week 10

I walk into the room full of friends and toys.
I play house with the other girls and boys.
I don't like the house made of wood.
I smash it around; ooh, it feels so good.

I make a house out of cardboard blocks.
I make the house with a BIG, BIG lock.
I feel so happy with my new home.
I don't feel sad; I feel safe to roam.

Me and my friends are having fun.
I don't have the feeling of wanting to run.
I am in the middle of a group of friends.
It's so much fun playing "pretend."

We play and sing and laugh at our jokes.
We pretend we are filling the house of wood with smoke.
There are sly little grins on all of the kids' faces.
We know we have burned up all the bad places.
We feel like we have learned there is no more pain.
We feel safe from harm; LET'S DO IT AGAIN!!
We reset the house made of wood.
We crash it down from where it stood.

The playroom is full of girls and boys.
The playroom is loud from us playing with toys.
Alone in the corner is a new little boy.
We wish he would enter our world full of joy.

He sits there looking around at the toys.
We know he doesn't know how to have fun . . .
We know he only wants to run.

We ask and plead for him to join in.
He sits all alone watching us play.
He wishes he could leave it for another day.

Closure

The last session of Play Therapy is here.
The boys and girls are wiping tears.
We are all one happy family.
No one really wants to leave.

We write each other notes of love,
The writings show how much we care.
All our hearts just want to share
How much it has meant, just being here.

We all have traveled down different roads,
We have met together, at a single path.
We have walked as a family for a short time,
We split again, much stronger inside.

The toys are placed on the shelves,
The wooden house is just a shell.
We say goodbye to the dolls and bears.
In our hearts, they will always be there.

We have learned there are others who care.
We know there is always love to share.
We now know how to laugh and cry,
We have found there are new things we want to try.

Our spirits are soaring, wanting to take wing.
We fly alone, but with family strings.
These close friends are family of our own,
But *this* family is healthy and strong.

We take what we've learned and put it to use.
We know we're okay, the strings we turn loose.
We fly alone, with the help of our friends.
Our love for each other is not "play pretend."

I will always love you wherever you may be.

Bobby !

—*Lois Hansen*

JACOB, 5

Without any introduction, Jacob picked up a 5-foot long stuffed snake, coiled it, and promptly placed it on the therapist's head. As the therapist calmly tracked this, Jacob backed up and began to shoot in her direction. She said, "I'm not for shooting." Jacob quickly responded, "I'm not shooting you; I'm shooting the snake!" The therapist already had been handcuffed and shot at, and had had a baby bottle placed near her mouth. It seemed natural to assume the next shot was for her, too, but Jacob had other plans.

—*Brenda Horton*

FRANKIE, 6

Therapist: "What do your parents argue about?"
Frankie: "About how sticky is the kitchen floor, and who is going to get stuck first."

—*Doris Omdahl*

DOUGLAS, 5

Douglas repeatedly tested limits in all 28 sessions. One day, while engaged in an activity about which he was doubtful, he asked, "Will you let me be *bad* in here?" When the therapist responded with "It sounds like you're not sure about that," Douglas (in his child's wisdom) sadly said, "My Mom would."

—*Anonymous*

JAMES

I have always wanted to know how to do everything right away and how to do it "right" the first time. Being a play therapist has taught me that there is no magic formula. I will be in a continual learning process forever, just like my clients. What a relief!

—*James Flowers*

ANNIE, 4

Annie had a most determined look as she pounded away at several of the reptiles and crustaceans. A small alligator bounced off the woodblock several times after Annie hit it. Finally, she put one handcuff on the alligator's neck and attached the other handcuff to a rope. Holding the rope on a shelf, Annie proceeded to pound on the alligator, saying, "Now, it can't get away. It can't jump off the stump."

—*Janet Brown*

DARLA, 8

I learn so much from my clients. Darla is a very quiet, reticent, and nonverbal child. One week I was sick and at the last minute had to cancel all of my play therapy sessions. The next week, I picked up Darla from her classroom. In all the previous sessions, she would smile at me shyly as we walked to the playroom; that day, however, Darla's eyes were fixed to the ground, her walk determined. As soon as the playroom door was closed, Darla turned straight to me, looked me in the eye, and said "You didn't pick me up." She then proceeded to shoot the dart gun all around the room and at *me*; she threw the ball, knocking over the paints—all unlike her previous sessions, where she tentatively touched a toy here and there or straightened the dollhouse quietly.

I realized something very important from Darla that day. Although she did not speak and never acknowledged my presence, the playroom and its experience were very important to her.

—*Kimberly Dillon*

MAXIE, 5

My son has been in play therapy with exciting results. Recently, as he was getting ready for his session, Maxie said that he could hardly wait to get to his session because "I have some serious playing to do!"

—*Anonymous*

KYLEE, 8

During four sessions of painting and other artwork, Kylee did not show evidence of any particularly important processing. As she had been with another therapist for quite a while, termination was being considered (without Kylee's knowledge). The very next session, Kylee tied me up with a rope, handcuffed me, and dressed me in glasses and a witch hat. She then proceeded to pile almost all of the toys around my feet, announcing that she was going to set the toys on fire and burn me up.

Later, Kylee's grandmother told me that they were involved in a big custody battle to have Kylee live with the grandparents. So, while I may not have seen what was being processed, there obviously was something that Kylee needed to work out and it didn't matter whether or not I knew what it was. *I was there to create a safe place for her to do it.*

—*Sherry Schultz*

JENNIE, 6

Entering the playroom for the first time, Jennie tentatively looked around. She sat down and did not approach any of the play materials. A few minutes later, Jennie said, "I know why I'm here. I'm here because I've been eating sand." After a few more minutes, she began to play. In the weeks that followed, Jennie's mother reported that Jennie always looked forward to her playroom time.

During the sixth session, Jennie sighed and said, "I just love to play." Then, she leaned closer to me and whispered, "I'm going to keep eating that sand so my Mom will bring me here."

—Debbie Killough

I walk in, afraid.
  Such a big room
  Such a big adult
Sitting in the corner.
  I feel so small.
I glance about the room,
  curious.
    I pick up a crown
    And place it on my
    head.
It makes me feel taller
    And I start to prance.
I smile to myself, pleased.
    The lady says I look
    proud
    And notices my crown and regal walk.
Boy, she must care . . .
    But I don't believe it.
I pick up the dart gun, plotting.
    I shoot at the wall
    Then I point it at *her*.
I bet she'll not like me now—
    I cock the trigger.
I watch her, smiling mischievously.
    Yet, she doesn't frown
    Or jump suddenly.
"I know you would like to do that,"
    She says calmly,
"But I'm not for shooting at."
"You can shoot the Bobo or the wall,"
    The lady in the corner suggests.
    Wow! I hadn't noticed the Bobo before.
I put on a mask
    And stalk the big thing.
Pow! Wham!! Bang!

That stupid Bobo's no match for me.
   Punch, kick, throw!
Whew, that feels really good.
   I feel a bit better.

"Five more minutes left in the playroom."
      There's so much left to do!
      Paint a house, make a garden,
Run around just to!
      I feel free and safe.
I walk out of the playroom, happy.
      Such a warm place—
      Such an understanding adult
Walking next to me.
      I feel peacefully in control.

                                —*Kimberly Dillon*

LINDY, 6

With a history of violent outbursts (hating everybody, everybody hating her, destroying property without remorse such as stabbing the kitchen wall with a butcher knife), sexual abuse between the ages of 2 and 4, hospitalization six months prior, and prescribed but unadministered Ritalin, Lindy came to my playroom.

In the first session, Lindy mentioned that she had been sexually abused, washed her hands, and engaged in aggressive activities. In the second session, she asked if we were going to talk about her "bad Daddy," but dropped the subject when I responded that it was up to her. Increasingly through the sessions, Lindy exhibited many aggressive and/or self-derogatory behaviors. In the sixth session, she spontaneously described the sexual abuse, and stated that she wished her "Daddy" was in jail.

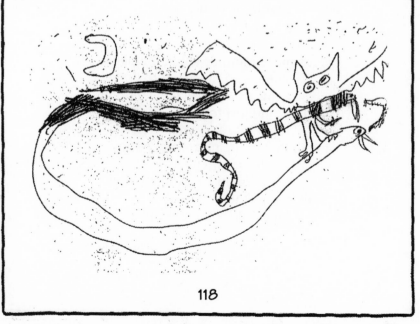

In the seventh session, Lindy drew a picture and then covered it with a lot of different colors, which she called a "storm." Putting on the black mask, she stated that she was a "bad man" and handcuffed the arms of a 3-foot rag doll behind its back. She picked up the rubber knife and attacked the doll, screaming "I hate you!", continuing to stab the doll and screaming that she was cutting off its arms and head. After several minutes, she reported that the doll was dead. She then removed the mask, reporting that she was a "good person," and unhandcuffed the doll and laid it on the couch so that her mother could find her and take her to the hospital. She then hugged the doll, stating over and over, "I love you!" and "I won't ever let anything happen to you." After 10 minutes, she reported that the doll was "okay" and laid it down on the couch. After 15 minutes of physically exhausting herself by kicking and hitting foam balls, she fixed a tea party for us, going into great detail to make sure plates and accessories were in appropriate places. Her behavior was very calm as she named each item she was serving. At the end of the session, my secretary reported that she had never seen Lindy so calm, since she usually was "bouncing" all over the waiting room. Mom also reported that Lindy was much calmer at home after that session.

In the next five sessions, Lindy was active but not as aggressive in her play; her play seemed to be more focused on current events. In the 12th and last session, Lindy put on the angel wings, halo, and king and queen crowns all together. She seemed to be very pleased with herself as she strutted around the room and stated that she was "special."

—*Margie Perry*

SALLY, 4

Sally shyly stood in front of the therapist and stated, "I have to go to the bathroom." The therapist reflected Sally's need and directed her toward the bathroom within the play therapy room. Even though this was a practicum setting with students observing, the therapist continued to track the behavior of the child in the bathroom. The funniest part was when the microphone magnified the sound of the child "relieving" herself and the sound of the toilet flushing.

—*Mary Sullivan*

BRADY, 6

Brady placed the handcuffs on me. I *felt* why handcuffs are used for relationship building. As he worked, Brady was physically close, and our eyes were on the same level. We concentrated on what he was doing, truly sharing the experience. I found that I enjoyed the experience as much as he seemed to enjoy it. I felt closer to him after we had shared this time. As I reviewed my tape, I could not *see* how I had changed in my relationship with Brady. No telltale flash crossed my face; no sirens screamed. Yet, somehow, I *knew* our relationship had grown significantly during those moments.

—*Sherry Jones*

CAROL, 7

After attending just two sessions of my play therapy class, I decided to change my language with the children I see regularly in my school counseling office. After I tracked Carol for about 10 minutes, she stopped, looked at me with awe, and said, "Gosh, you must be psychotic [psychic]!" I just chuckled to myself and continued to track her amazement.

—*Terri Evensvold*

JORDIN, 7

During Jordin's 10th session, the patterns of past sessions were in full swing. She held the flashlight while standing at the far end of the room and asked, "Would you turn the lights off?" I gave my response: "Oh, you would really like for me to turn the lights off." Jordin replied, "Yeah! Turn 'em off!" only to have the responsibility turned back to her with my saying, "I can tell you would really like for me to do that, but that's something you can do." In past sessions, this usually would result in Jordin turning the lights off. This time, however, she sighed, put her hands on her hips, and said, "I know that's something I can do, but that's something *you* can do, too!"

—*Tommy Wilbeck*

ELISE, 5

In a session with Elise, I was reminded of the importance of not labeling toys. Taking the ray gun from the shelf and aiming it into a pot on the stove, Elise shot the gun while making sounds and sparkling lights. As I tracked with "You're getting that . . . and now, you're doing that . . . ," Elise expanded on my tracking with "I am hypnotizing the soup." If I had either labeled the gun or said, "You are shooting the gun into that pot," I might have blocked Elise from fully expressing herself!

—Lynda Lynk

DANNY, 7

I found out how easy it is to miss the point. The subtlety of the child's world in context, when he is being still, is amazing. To Danny, as he stood silent with his decision to do so, it must have seemed like I was shouting to him from far away. I was wanting him *to do something*, attending to him with an air of anticipation while *his "doing"* filled the room to overflowing. *I* was waiting for the sound of him, and *he* was defining the interval in between, the silence without which there can be no music.

—Paul Pendery

SCOTT AND DREW, 6

I see twins, Scott and Drew, together one day a week. In our fifth session, Drew began to emulate his abusive father and was doing a great deal of acting out with aggressive toys and verbal remarks to his twin brother. Drew proceeded to handcuff Scott to my rocking chair. Scott was very cooperative and as soon as the handcuffs were closed, Scott said, "Oh, Drew, I wish I could stay in this room for always. I feel so good here." Drew stopped his play, grabbed another set of handcuffs, and said, "Good idea; so do I." As tears came to my eyes, I observed the bond between Drew and Scott. They sat silently for awhile until Drew said, "We'll be good dads, won't we? Hey, let's play fast 'cause we gotta go before they start to the lunchroom!"

—*Sheila Lilley*

TERRENCE, 8

Not a word had been spoken by Terrence for the entire session. I sat there in my chair watching him dress up in a button-up shirt and some cowboy boots to go along with the blue jeans he already had on. As I continued to reflect what he was doing and what I could see, an overwhelming feeling came over me. I was in awe of the process. I could not believe that so much could be said without a word being spoken. It did not matter that the clothes were too small or that Terrence had other clothes on underneath. This was Terrence and who he wanted to be at that moment. A look of pride and satisfaction came over his face, and as I reflected those feelings to him, he continued to walk around the room as if he were a new person. Words do not need to be spoken and conversation does not need to take place in order for a relationship to be built!

—*Tom Stevens*

ALISHA, 3

Alisha allegedly had been sexually abused. She had disclosed several things in the play therapy sessions, but Child Protective Services would never investigate because of her age. I was so hoping Alisha would begin to get as angry at the system as I was. One day in a play therapy session, Alisha took a doll and began to shoot it in the ear with a gun. I stated in my most empathic/reflective voice, "You must really be angry." Alisha turned to me and stated impatiently, "NO! She's getting her ears pierced!"

—*Carolyn Adams*

HAYLEY, 9

One day I received a call from Hayley's troubled father. He was angry and stated that he *MUST* talk to me before Hayley's session. Hayley's school principal had called the father in to confront Hayley with her father present. Seemingly, Hayley had been passing around "dirty" notes, so the principal asked Hayley why she had written the notes and what she thought of herself. Hayley looked at the principal and matter-of-factly stated, "Well, I'm going to play therapy today, and, in there, I can do *anything* I want!" Hayley's father said that he almost died of embarrassment and wanted to know if it was true and what did I have to say about it. Being on the spot, I felt like sliding down in my chair and did not know whether to laugh or cry; however, I calmly replied, "Well, she's partly right; she can do *many* of the things she would like." I went on to explain the difference, and he did not say anything more.

—*Phyllis Butsch*

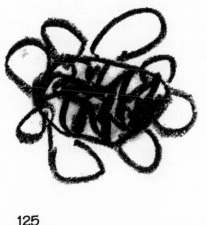

CALICO

Over a 6-week period, I had the privilege of observing a young cat give birth to and take care of her first litter of kittens. As I watched her with her kittens, I was awed by her loving, gentle ways with the life she had brought forth. Calico was ever-patient, soft-voiced, playful, and yet guiding. The one thing, however, that caught my attention and my imagination was the nondirective play Calico allowed her kittens. She also set limits. The kittens were never out of her sight, but, unless she sensed that they might come into harm's way, she did not interfere with their play. As I watched this little cat family, I thought to myself that if humans could lead such a simple life, there would be no need for me to provide play therapy.

Life for the human species is not simple, however, and there is a need for therapists to help those who have gotten off track to get back on track. It is most helpful to do this when human life is still at the beginning, when play is the primary means of communication.

My point of view is that client/child-centered play therapy is the most appropriate approach in helping a person along to living a healthful and satisfying life. I believe in remaining unobtrusive, gentle, interested, respectful, and totally accepting (like the mother cat) of the client as s/he is, intervening only to keep the client (and/or myself) from harm's way.

—*Margaret Vaughn–Foerster*

TERRY, 8

In our last session, I heard a sob as Terry lay face down in the sandbox. "It sounds like you are sad." With eyes downcast and voice low, Terry remarked, "I've heard about people crying at weddings, but not about leaving the playroom."

—*Susan Corley*

Dear Judy,
Thank You For
Helping Me With
Making My Own
Disitions In You
Room. You Made
Me Feel More
Comfotable.

Love
Alice

—*Judi Gilbert*